CITYSPOTS
HANOVER

D0525927

WHAT'S IN YOUR GUIDEBOOK?

Independent authors Impartial up-to-date information from our travel experts who meticulously source local knowledge.

Experience Thomas Cook's 165 years in the travel industry and guidebook publishing enriches every word with expertise you can trust.

Travel know-how Thomas Cook has thousands of staff working around the globe, all living and breathing travel.

Editors Travel-publishing professionals, pulling everything together to craft a perfect blend of words, pictures, maps and design.

You, the traveller We deliver a practical, no-nonsense approach to information, geared to how you really use it.

CITYSPOTS
HANOVER

Written by Whitney Love
Updated by Miguel Montfort

Published by Thomas Cook Publishing
A division of Thomas Cook Tour Operations Limited
Company registration No: 1450464 England
The Thomas Cook Business Park, 9 Coningsby Road
Peterborough PE3 8SB, United Kingdom
Email: books@thomascook.com, Tel: +44 (0)1733 416477
www.thomascookpublishing.com

Produced by The Content Works Ltd
Aston Court, Kingsmead Business Park, Frederick Place
High Wycombe, Bucks HP11 1LA
www.thecontentworks.com

Series design based on an original concept by Studio 183 Limited

ISBN: 978-1-84848-044-5

First edition © 2007 Thomas Cook Publishing
This second edition © 2009 Thomas Cook Publishing
Text © Thomas Cook Publishing
Maps © Thomas Cook Publishing/PCGraphics (UK) Limited
Transport map © Communicarta Limited

Series Editor: Lucy Armstrong
Production/DTP: Steven Collins

Printed and bound in Spain by GraphyCems

Cover photography (Kramerstrasse, Altstadt) © f1 online/Alamy

CONTENTS

SYMBOLS KEY

The following symbols are used throughout this book:

ⓐ address ⓣ telephone ⓦ website address ⓛ opening times
ⓝ public transport connections ⓘ important

The following symbols are used on the maps:

i	information office	▪	points of interest
✈	airport	O	city
✚	hospital	O	large town
🛡	police station	○	small town
▤	bus station	═	motorway
▤	railway station	—	main road
U	U-Bahn	····	minor road
✝	cathedral	—	railway
❶	numbers denote featured cafés & restaurants		

Hotels and restaurants are graded by approximate price as follows:
£ budget price **££** mid-range price **£££** expensive

In addresses, 'Strasse' and '-strasse' (meaning 'street' or 'road')
are abbreviated to 'Str.' and '-str.'; 'Platz' and '-platz' (meaning
'square') are abbreviated to 'Pl.' and '-pl.'

● *The reflective majesty of the Neues Rathaus*

Introduction

Hanover is one of Germany's up-and-coming cities – for its larger-than-life trade fairs, gardens, festivals and cultural institutions. In recent years it has grown in status by hosting World Expo 2000 and the 2006 FIFA World Cup.

Hanover is also a rising star on the tourism scene for Germans themselves, due to its laid-back, chilled-out nature. Smart casual isn't just a way to dress in Hanover, it's a mentality embraced along with a love for all things green. Hanoverians are a very active, sporty bunch and focus more on what they can *do* with friends and family than on what they can *see*.

Most of the half-a-million residents of Hanover have a deeply rooted, almost fanatical admiration for the city and their fellow citizens. They truly appreciate what's on offer and take full advantage of activities and festivals – especially during the summer.

By many accounts, 70 per cent of Hanover was destroyed by the Allied bombings during World War II. When much of the city was rebuilt, it was done so for functionality – not form and design. Tourists should focus less on the visual candy, and more on things to get out and do. Don't misinterpret – there are beautiful treasures inside and outside the city limits, but you'll find your travel schedule packed with things to *do*, not just *see*.

Local culture is also very aware of its royal past and links to Great Britain. You will be as well, before you leave town. Hochdeutsch, or High German, is spoken as the regional language. This is the clearest-sounding German you'll hear in Germany, so enjoy it for all its worth.

With all that is on offer, it is no wonder that Hanover is growing in popularity as a must-see German city.

◔ *City view from the Altes Rathaus*

When to go

If your primary concern is the weather, the balmiest times in Hanover are the sunny summer months of July and August. As well as rain, spring also ushers in the major international trade fairs, when the city swells by at least 50,000 visitors for CeBIT alone; you'll know it by the number that seem to be getting on your tram, and if you're not visiting specifically to attend one of these events, you may find the city rather crowded. Even if you can't make it out to the Messe, the main exhibition centre, many companies offer free give-aways and promotional products at the Hauptbahnhof (main railway station) and Kröpcke (Hanover's central square). When major trade fairs are in town, ÜSTRA offers more S-Bahn trains (regional trains) from Laatzen and the Messe to the main railway station. If you want to chill out without freezing

● *Café life in the Altstadt*

to death, autumn is a popular time for sitting outdoors at cafés and enjoying the kick-off to the cultural season.

But there's no bad time to visit the city: the warmth of the welcome never changes, the sights and attractions are stunning all year long and Hanover is always open for fun.

SEASONS & CLIMATE

The weather can range from comfortably warm and mildly humid to hot and unbearably muggy. Temperatures usually drop in late August to early September. During December, January and February snow is common, but snowfall is lighter than in other regions. Spring is usually quite wet – so bring an umbrella.

ANNUAL EVENTS

March
CeBIT Raking in almost 500,000 visitors every year, this is the world's largest tech trade fair – electronic gadgets galore. Tickets may be hard to come by so get yours early!
Ⓦ www.cebit.de/besucherservice

May
Herrenhausen Festival Weeks Features top-class classical concerts. Various weeks in late May, June, July and August.
Ⓦ www.festwochen-herrenhausen.de
Herrenhäusen Gärten Illuminations Admire the illuminations while listening to baroque music.
International Fireworks Competition, **Grosser Garten** Watch the world's top pyrotechnists battle for the title of 'world's best'. Plus cabaret acts and live music.

MASALA Festival Music from around the world, sponsored by the Pavillon (see page 74). Ⓦ www.masala-festival.de

June
Jazzfestival Open-air jazz music event on the steps of the Neues Rathaus (see page 66). ❶ 454 455 Ⓦ www.jazz-club.de
A Terrific Weekend Expo and **The NDR 2 Plaza Festival** These events are usually held in early to mid-June at the Messe (see page 94).
Schützenfest Hannover Attend one of the summer's largest events and practise your *Lüttje Lage* skills (see page 14).

July
Classical Music in the Old Town Groups from all over Germany play classical music and you can listen for free Ⓝ U-Bahn: Markthalle
Little Festival in the Great Garden Small-scale performing arts, music and drama on 30 stages around the Grosser Garten (see page 77).
Reincarnation Parade Techno-infused music event similar to the Love Parade in Berlin. Held between late July and mid-August. Ⓦ www.reincarnation-parade.de/

August
Maschseefest End the summer festival season with a big bang and sand between your toes! Many of the local bars offer a beach version of their hard-floored originals. Rides, entertainment acts, concerts and mounds of food and drink on offer.
Steinhude Festive Weekend Held on the last weekend of the month, this climaxes with a spectacular fireworks display that lights up the lake at Steinhuder Meer (see page 90).

Late September/early October
Schützenplatz Oktoberfest One of the largest Oktoberfests in northern Germany with free admission. ☎ 131 70 35 ⓦ www.oktoberfest-hannover.de

Late November/December
Up-and-coming International Film Festival Hanover Biennial film festival (held in odd years) showcasing some of the best filmmakers. ☎ 661 102 ⓦ www.up-and-coming.de
Weihnachtsmärkte Various Christmas markets open. The largest are at the Hauptbahnhof, Kröpcke and in the Altstadt.

PUBLIC HOLIDAYS
New Year's Day 1 Jan
Good Friday 10 Apr 2009; 2 Apr 2010; 22 Apr 2011
Easter Sunday 12 Apr 2009; 4 Apr 2010; 24 Apr 2011
Easter Monday 13 Apr 2009; 5 Apr 2010; 25 Apr 2011
Labour Day 1 May
Whit Monday first Mon in June
Pentecost 7 June 2009; 23 May 2010; 12 June 2011
Corpus Christi 11 June 2009; 3 June 2010; 23 June 2011
Day of German Unity 3 Oct
Christmas Day 25 Dec
Boxing Day 26 Dec
New Year's Eve 31 Dec

Schützenfest Hannover

What do you get when you take one part archery and marksmen events, two parts traditional pomp and circumstance, then mix together with two heaping scoops of *Lüttje Lage* and food, plus a dash of live music? Hanover's Schützenfest, the largest marksmen event in the world and one of the annual festivals that make Hanover a hotbed of merriment for locals and visitors. It dates back to the 17th century and is as much a part of the local culture here as Oktoberfest is in Munich. The event usually occurs in late June to early July.

Schützenfest jumps off each year with the free-to-attend riflemen's parade, the longest procession in Europe. This colourful, yet traditional parade includes over 150 local clubs and social groups who dance and march through the city centre.

When at the fest, don't miss *Lüttje Lage*, a drink that is as special for the way it is consumed as it is for its flavour. Enjoying this adventuresome beverage begins by holding a small glass each of *Lüttje Lage* beer and *Korn Schnapps* between your fingers, one on the back of each hand, then pouring the *Schnapps* into the beer. When both liquids are in the same glass, you drink. What begins as two, ends up as one with a small flick of the fingers and lots of practice. Fascinating to watch – this trick takes years to master. Look for the men in shiny top-hats, suits and white gloves to show you how.

Besides enjoying the fun of *Lüttje Lage*, the exhilarating carnival rides at Schützenfest offer visitors more entertainment. Queue up for the standards – bumper cars and Ferris wheel –

or something more adventurous and gravity defying. Carnival rides not your thing? Look no further than the entertainment stages or to the marksmen events themselves.

For more information, visit Ⓦ www.schuetzenfest-hannover.de

🔺 *Join the drummers at Schützenfest Hannover*

History

The city of Hanover (Hannover in its German spelling) began, as do many cities along rivers, as a trading post for travelling merchants to buy and sell goods. However, while the first settlement in the Hanover area was established in 950, the earliest official records of 'Honovere', later called 'Hannover', date the city back to 1150, with the city charter dating to almost 100 years later. Over the next 300 years, Hanover saw major advancements in its development, namely, the construction of its massive city wall, plus its first major buildings such as the Kreuz, Aegidien and Markt churches. This period was also highlighted by a small but important invention by Cord Broyhan – a light beer, which not only gave the locals something to sip during their medieval happy hour but also helped stimulate the city's economy.

Later, Hanover became a Protestant city and in 1625 was occupied by Danish troops as a part of the Thirty Years' War. During this same phase, a third of the population died of the plague. In the next century, the Duke of Calenberg came to town and decided to set up shop. Later known as the Duke of Hanover, he commissioned the massive kitchen garden, now known as the Herrenhäuser Gärten, from Michael Grosse. Gottfried Wilhelm Leibniz was counsellor and librarian to the ducal court. Duke Ernst August was made Elector and Hanover became the capital of the electorate of Brunswick-Lüneburg.

Things really began to get 'royal' in 1701 when electress Sophia was declared the successor to the British throne. Ten years later, after her death, Georg Ludwig, descendant of the

Duke of Hanover, ascended the British throne, becoming George I of Great Britain and Ireland. Hanoverian rule in Great Britain and Ireland lasted until 1837.

In 1803, after Napoleon imposed the Convention of Artlenburg, about 30,000 French soldiers occupied the electorate of Hanover. France occupied Hanover for the next ten years. At the Congress of Vienna, the Kingdom of Hanover was born with the help of George III. In 1866, during the Austro-Prussian War, Hanover was taken over by the Prussians, King George V fled and Hanover became the Prussian royal seat.

Between 1934 and 1939, the Maschsee was constructed by the National Socialists (NSDAP). In the last years of World War II, more than half the city was destroyed in over 100 Allied air raids. At the end of the war, Hanover became the capital of Lower Saxony, rebuilt itself and opened the Medizinische Hochschule Hannover. Since 1989, Hanover has spent much of its efforts as a city polishing and buffing up its 'new' look with the help of revenue derived from EXPO 2000, the 2006 FIFA World Cup and the CeBIT trade fair.

Hanover's success as one of the hosts of 2006's FIFA World Cup created a feel-good factor that has simply never dissolved. The same year saw the election of a new Lord Mayor (*Oberbürgermeister*), Stephan Weil. In 2008, he led an initiative to strengthen ties with the city's Muslim population. This was a typically inclusive gesture from a man who plans to promote Hanover's commitment to cultural diversity as it positions itself as one of Germany's most progressive cities.

Lifestyle

Hanover is a family and tourist friendly city in love with itself. Ask local residents for their opinion of their home town and 80 per cent of them will tell you they would never want to live anywhere else. Why? Hanover is a city that nicely straddles urban and provincial life, and with charm. From the uber-cool hub of Linden and the city centre to the lushly green wide-open spaces, Hanover has a bit of something for almost everyone. With a moderate cost of

⬤ *Gateway to the horticultural delights of the Grosser Garten*

living and expanding economic prospects, many here enjoy a comfortable lifestyle.

Hanoverians like to work hard and play hard. While most people dress more causally at work than their counterparts in Hamburg and Berlin, work and business are taken as seriously as anywhere else. 'Smart casual' is the normal uniform when going out, except for special occasions and in some nightspots and restaurants.

While it is not true of all inhabitants, Hanoverians are very aware of their royal historical association with the British throne. Combine that with the typical aloof and reserved northern German mentality and what you get is a slightly odd mix, which sometimes catches newcomers off guard. Don't be fooled! In general, most of the local residents are friendly and open, especially to visitors. Many of the locals speak English and some speak French, Russian, Turkish or Polish.

Locals love anything green and frantically race outside at the first hint of sunny weather. Places like the Maschsee, Eilenriede, the Hartz Mountains and the Steinhuder Meer are much frequented recreation spots – especially at the weekend. In summer, you'll often find a weekend festival to attend.

Trade fairs tend to affect the whole city. When a large trade fair is in town, many hotels and some restaurants nearly double their prices. Likewise, restaurants may switch to menus that offer fewer dining options but stay open longer to accommodate the crowds. Also, public transport becomes uncomfortably overcrowded. ÜSTRA and Deutsche Bahn help alleviate some of the madness by offering more regional trains from Hannover Messe/Laatzen station to the main railway station, Hauptbahnhof.

Culture

Generally speaking, the cultural scene in Hanover has many things to see and to experience. Although the city has a reputation for being slightly on the provincial side, the cultural offerings are plentiful given the number of inhabitants in the area, and many of these offerings are considered on a par with the best in Germany, and further afield.

Hanover is a city drenched in outdoor and indoor art. Many of the city's streets are decked out in high style with ornamental eye candy – enough to make a city twice its size blush. The streets are decorated with expressive statues, art forms, installations and structures. Besides the Skulpturenmeile and Nanas (see page 66), have a look at the outdoor art that's dotted about Kröpcke, Lister Meile and Aegidientorplatz.

Museums here are top-notch and hold some of the best collections in Europe. They are frequented by Hanoverians of all ages and classes, including school groups who all love their museums and spend time making the most of them – especially when it rains. Most museums are closed on Mondays, and admission is free one day of the week.

The State Opera in Hanover is considered one of the best in the world. It not only attracts great singers and musicians but has a large local following. Annual season tickets often sell out and same-day tickets can be hard to come by. If you plan on attending a show, be sure to buy tickets well in advance or risk missing out.

◗ *A promise of a choice of theatre performances*

The ballet of the State Opera is also housed in the Opernhaus (opera house) and is said to be one of the best in Germany. Programmes of events are available at the Opernhaus ticket office.

The **Opera house** (ⓐ Opernhaus Opernpl. 1 ☎ 999 911 11 ⓦ www.oper-hannover.de) itself is one of the focal points of the city centre and gorgeous when illuminated at night. Built between 1845 and 1852 in the late classical style by Georg Ludwig Friedrich Laves, it was almost completely destroyed during the Allied air raids of World War II. Since its resurrection in 1950, it has undergone more facelifts. Located behind Kröpcke, the *Platz* in front of the opera house is commonly the stage for political rallies.

Theatre in Hanover is good, but not for those who don't speak German. Show information can be found in the tourist information office (see page 137) and at the venue itself. Head to the **Schauspielhaus** (ⓐ Prinzenstr. 9 ☎ 999 911 11 ⓦ www.staatstheater-hannover.de), **Theater am Aegi** (ⓐ Aegidientorpl. 2 ☎ 989 33 33 ⓦ www.theater-am-aegi.de) and **GOP Varieté** (ⓐ Georgstr. 36 ☎ 301 86 76 ⓦ www.variete.de).

● *Historic Hanover: Kramerstrasse in Altstadt*

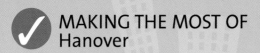

Shopping

The shopping options in Hanover leave much to be desired, both for tourists and for locals. Basic items and standard staples are easily found, but much else is not. There are a few designer clothes shops, most centred around Luisestrasse and some speciality boutiques for clothing and other items sprinkled throughout the city. To give your wallet a workout, visit Galerie Luise (see page 48), Kröpcke, Lister Meile, Lindener Marktplatz and the hip student-friendly boutiques on Engelbosteler Damm.

Vintage clothing can be found at **Kleidermarkt** (ⓐ Lister Meile), a national chain of vintage and used clothing stores where you can buy clothing by the kilo. Look out for Wednesday's special, where items are about 30 per cent cheaper.

Open-air food and flea markets are as much of the Hanover experience as the Nanas. Low priced, but high quality and sometimes organic fruit and vegetables and other foodstuffs, can be found on Saturdays at **Lindener Marktplatz, Am Klagesmarkt** (also on Wednesdays) and various other neighbourhood shopping areas. Open-air food markets operate from early until at least 12.00, usually 13.00.

The largest weekend flea markets are located on the Leine and near the University, opening 07.00–16.00. The Deutsche Messe (see page 91) also often hosts a weekend flea market.

Open-air markets and flea markets are the only places where haggling is acceptable, and sometimes required.

When in season, locals buy *Spargel*, or white asparagus. The white asparagus season causes a panic-like frenzy and the pale spearheaded darlings show up on most local menus. Most of

Germany's *Spargel* crop is grown in Lower Saxony and it is common for the local population to buy massive amounts at the end of the season to freeze at home and use throughout the year.

⬛ *Passerelle – a good place to shop*

USEFUL SHOPPING PHRASES

What time do the shops open/close?
Um wieviel Uhr öffnen/schließen die Geschäfte?
Oom veefeel oor erffnen/shleessen dee geshefter?

How much is this?
Wieviel kostet das?
Veefeel kostet das?

Can I try this on?
Kann ich das anprobieren?
Can ikh das anprobeeren?

My size is ...
Ich habe Größe ...
Ikh haber grerser ...

I'll take this one, thank you
Ich nehme das, danke schön
Ikh neymer das, danker shern

This is too large/too small/too expensive
Es ist zu groß/zu klein/zu teuer
Es ist tsu gross/tsu kline/tsu toyer

The only Sunday shopping in town is at the train station. Lidl and Rossmann will help you get sorted with all the lotion, soap, bread and drinks you can manage to carry out.

The best place in town to buy souvenirs is at the tourist information office or one of the major department stores in the centre of town. Although the tourist information office has less on offer, the prices are lower and the quality is on a par with more expensive shops.

Eating & drinking

Hanoverians, like most Germans, start their day with breakfast, eaten between 07.00 and 09.00 and the most standard feature is, you guessed it, an assortment of breads or *Brötchen* (rolls). This is followed by cold cuts, cheeses, marmalades, chocolate spreads, butter and other dairy or meat-based spreads. Sometimes a cooked egg is also included. All washed down with a few cups of coffee or tea and sometimes juice. If this doesn't appeal, yoghurt and fruit should usually be on offer.

Many Hanoverians have switched to eating lighter fare at lunch or smaller portions of more traditional meals. Lunch menus in Hanover more commonly reflect influences from Holland, Italy, France and the Nordic countries. Look for eateries and *Imbiss* (snack or light meal) stands outside of the city centre if you want food with more flavour, flair and culinary fun.

Many restaurants switch to menus with slightly larger, richer portions at dinnertime. Most locals eat dinner between 18.00 and 20.00.

In general, the same spots that are open for lunch are also open for dinner, but there are exceptions. However, most establishments

PRICE CATEGORIES

The price ratings given in this book indicate the approximate cost of a three-course meal for one person, excluding drinks.

£ up to €20   ££ €20–40   £££ over €40

that open for breakfast close after lunch. Many places close between lunch and dinner, so plan ahead if you like to eat lunches late, or dinners early.

Tipping can be a tricky matter for most since, by German law, the price of all meals must include a service charge. Giving a gratuity is simply *Trinkgeld*, i.e. 'money for drinks after work'. However optional tipping may be, it is slightly expected for half-decent service. For anything under €5, round off to the nearest euro. For €5–20, round up the next nearest euro and throw in another euro if the service was exceptional. For anything up to €50, round off to the nearest €5 or €10, but usually not more than €3–5 for the entire bill. Fifty euros and above, round off to the nearest €10 mark.

Children are welcome in neighbourhood restaurants but usually not in fancy or slick, uber-cool restaurants in the city centre. Call ahead to ask for high chairs and children's menus if a little one will accompany you.

Picnicking is common, especially in summer. Visit one of the local discount supermarkets such as Aldi for cheaper-priced basics, full-service supermarkets for better quality and a wider selection, and speciality markets for the *crème de la crème* foodstuffs; open-air food markets operate mid-week and on Saturdays. The best places for a picnic are in the Herrenhäuser Gärten (see page 77), near the Neues Rathaus (see page 66) or any city park.

What Hanover lacks in local food specialities, it makes up for in enthusiasm. Cuisine is more regional than anything else, with local growers and producers from the whole of the Hanover region and Lower Saxony bringing their goods to the city. Smoked eel from the North Sea and especially *Spargel*, or white asparagus, dominate menus when in season. *Spargel* is normally eaten

USEFUL DINING PHRASES

I would like a table for ... people, please
Ein Tisch für ... Personen, bitte
Ine teesh foor ... perzohnen, bitter

Waiter/waitress!
Herr Ober/Frau Kellnerin!
Hair ohber/frow kell-nair-in!

May I have the bill, please?
Die Rechnung, bitte?
Dee rekhnung, bitter?

I am a vegetarian. Does this contain meat?
Ich bin Vegetarier (Vegetarierin fem.).
Enthält das hier Fleisch?
Ish bin veggetaareer (veggetaareerin).
Enthelt dass heer flyshe?

Where is the toilet (restroom) please?
Wo sind die Toiletten, bitte?
Voo zeent dee toletten, bitter?

I would like a cup of/two cups of/another coffee/tea, please
Eine Tasse/Zwei Tassen/noch eine Tasse Kaffee/Tee, bitte
Iner tasser/tsvy tassen/nok iner tasser kafey/tey, bitter

I would like a beer/two beers, please
Ein Bier/Zwei Biere, bitte
Ine beer/tsvy beerer, bitter

with thinly sliced Parma-like ham on the side and drenched in butter or hollandaise sauce.

Hanover has only a few remaining breweries, namely Herrenhausen, Gilde and Brauhaus Ernst August. It is also home to the *Broyhan*, a well-known beer invented by Cord Broyhan in the 16th century, although no longer available in its original form: back then, it was a top-fermented pale wheat beer, similar to *Berliner Weisse*. One local type of beer still being brewed is *Lüttje Lage*, a dark, top-fermented beer available from Gilde and Herrenhausen.

⬥ *Let's raise a glass or two*

Entertainment & nightlife

The key to finding a good club, bar or pub in Hanover is your keen sense of being in the right place on the right night, at the right time of the evening. Most clubs are open seven days a week, but are patronised only on Fridays and Saturdays, with some hip-hopping away on Thursdays. Most of the action begins at 23.00, with clubs maxing out at 02.00 and lasting until dawn or until the last person leaves, usually 06.00.

Most bars are open with the same frequency – low attendance until the weekend. Pubs, especially the Irish and English ones, normally include one or two table quiz and karaoke nights.

Hanover has one well-known jazz venue, Jazz Club Hannover (see page 88), which is worth a visit. It attracts acts from Germany and the world over.

Open-air events are frequent in summer and early autumn. Popular music concerts are usually held at the TUI Arena (see page 34), Faust (see page 88) and Pavillon (see page 74). Tickets can be found at the venues themselves or online at ⓦ www.hannover-concerts.de

Street performers are common in Hanover, but leave much to be desired.

As to the best theatre options, try the Theater am Aegi (see page 22) for details of shows or more information. Hanover also has smaller theatre venues and troupes, but dates and shows can be more sporadic. Check local listings in the German-language *Prinz* magazine for more information. The University of Hanover has an English-language theatre troupe that offers respectable shows twice a year, at very reasonable prices.

Hanover has several cinemas showing films in English as well as art house films. Check out the Apollo Kino on Limmerstrasse in Linden (see page 89) for some of the most inspired offerings. The cinema is one of the oldest continuously running independent ones in Germany, dating back to the 1920s, and has most of its original décor.

Foreign films shown in one of Hanover's two multiplexes are usually not screened in the original language, except at special times during the week or month depending upon popularity. In general, they are dubbed.

As well as professional classical music concerts, the local **Music School** (ⓦ www.hmt-hannover.de) puts on highly enjoyable programming, at a lower price. Free classical events are also offered by the city in the Altstadt throughout the year.

Opera performances in Hanover are highly regarded. Buy tickets either at the ticket office at the opera house (see page 22) or from the tourist information office.

Dancing its way into the hearts of admirers is the Ballettensembles Hannover, the local state-sponsored ballet group. The season usually begins in late autumn/early winter and tickets can be found at the opera house.

Hanover has no English-language event listings. Be brave and try the German-language options – you should be able to manage. Most ticket office staff speak at least some English (especially with all of the international visitors traipsing in and out of the city) and most venues have websites.

◀ *The opera house illuminated at dusk*

Sport & relaxation

SPECTATOR SPORTS

Tickets can be hard to come by for the well-supported Hannover 96 football club, known as The Reds (ⓐ AWD Arena, Arthur-Menge-Ufer 5 ⓦ www.hannover96.de), but can be bought from the ticket office at the stadium in advance or sometimes on the same day. Tickets can also be bought in the city centre at ⓐ Nordmannpassage 6 or online at ⓦ www.uestra-reisen.de

Hanover is home to two ice hockey teams – the Scorpions and the Indians: both teams have made it to division play-offs in recent years. The Scorpions play at **TUI Arena** (ⓐ Expo Plaza 7 ⓦ www.tui-arena.de), which can be reached via U-Bahn line 6 to Messe/Ost. The Indians play at the **Eisstadion am Pferdeturm** (ⓐ Am Pferdeturm 7 ⓦ www.hannover-indians.de ⓝ U-Bahn: Kantplatz). Tickets to see both teams can be bought from the tourist information office, or on venue and team websites. Hanover also has a local basketball team, the UBC Hannover Tigers. Games are usually held on the **University campus** and tickets are available at the venue (ⓐ Uni-Dome, Am Moritzwinkel ⓦ www.ubc-hannover.de).

PARTICIPATION SPORTS

Hanoverians take full advantage of the city's numerous bike paths, hiking locations and, especially, the walking paths in the **Eilenriede forest**. This is Europe's largest city forest at 650 ha (1,600 acres) (ⓝ U-Bahn: Zoo, then walk east).

Hanoverians, and you, can also get a green fix on the **Maschsee**, a man-made lake built in the 1930s. Come here for warm-weather activities such as riverboat tours, paddleboats and sunbathing in summer, and ice skating in winter (Bus: 131/132, Sprengel Museum).

● *Sailing on the Maschsee*

Head south of the Maschsee to **Ricklinger Teiche** for fewer crowds, picnicking, biking and the nearby Ricklinger Aegir-Bad, a city pool. Tram: 3, 7, 17 to Beekestrasse; it's a long walk from the tram stop though, so bike it if you can.

RELAXATION
Cycling
Der Grüne Ring (The Green Ring) is a series of short, medium and longer length bike trails all over the city and surrounding region – enjoy one or more of the numerous bike trails mentioned in the Green Ring tour booklet and maps. Maps are available at most bike shops or from the tourist information office. www.gruener-ring-hannover.de lists trails but is in German only.

Werkstatt Treff Vahreheide Bicycles can be rented from Hanover main railway station for about €6 per day or €25 per week. The workshop also carries out bike repairs. Lilienthalstr. 12 633 293

Golf
The Hanover region has 16 golf courses, mostly located outside the city, and are more easily accessible if you have your own transport. Most courses rent clubs, etc. The nearest ones are:
Golfclub Langenhagen e.V. Hainhaus 22, Langenhagen 736 832 www.golfclublangenhagen.de
Golfclub Hannover e.V. Am Blauen See 120, Garbsen (05157) 730 68 www.golfclub-hannover.de
Golfclub Gleidingen Am Golfpl. 1, Laatzen-Gleidungen (05102) 30 11 www.golf-gleidingen.de

Accommodation

Hanover is generally a safe place to stay, and accommodation is available throughout the city. With the world's largest trade fair grounds, Hanover offers more types of accommodation than most cities of a similar size. Also, many locals open their homes to the onslaught of guests that arrive every year for major events, especially CeBIT and the other industry trade fairs.

When possible, book in advance: although accommodation can be found by walking in off the street quite easily most of the year, hotels near the city centre, Deutsche Messe and Nordstadt book up quickly, especially if a trade fair or special event is on. For bookings, contact the tourist office (see page 137).

During trade fair time, prices rise alarmingly. Many establishments not only raise their prices – some almost double their rates. They also reduce the hotel shuttle schedules.

Many of the smaller towns and villages that surround Hanover have quaint and comfy bed and breakfasts or inns for visitors. If you have a car, or feel comfortable navigating the sometimes sporadic public transport, these options can be a nice alternative.

PRICE CATEGORIES

The ratings below indicate the approximate cost of a double room including breakfast per person per night during the high season or during trade fairs.

£ up to €100   ££ €100–200   £££ over €200

The city also has a few B&Bs and inns, mostly near the Eilenriede and in the Zoo and Anderten quarters.

Apartments are also available; minimum 3–7-day stay. Try Hannover Apartment World ⓐ Hallerstr. 19 ⓦ hannover.apartment-world.de

⬤ *The budget City Hotel on Thielenplatz*

HOTELS

Bei Hölzchen £ Join the Raabe family for their warm and gracious hospitality. Near to the Deutsche Messe. ⓐ Peiner Str. 87 (City Centre) ❶ 984 69 60 ⓦ www.beihoelzchen.de ⓝ Bus 128: Elsenborner Strasse

City Hotel am Thielenplatz £ The perfect choice for staying in the city centre. ⓐ Thielenpl. 2 (City Centre) ❶ 327 691 ⓦ www.smartcityhotel.de ⓝ U-Bahn: Thielenplatz/Schauspielhaus

Haus Sparkuhl Hotel Garni £ Frau Scholvin and staff offer a cosy family-run hotel one stop from the main railway station. ⓐ Hischestr. 4 (City Centre) ❶ 937 80 ⓦ www.hotel-sparkuhl.de ⓝ U-Bahn: Werderstrasse

Hotel Savoy £ The breakfast room is reminiscent of summers on the English coast. Eighteen-room hotel near the centre of town. ⓐ Schlosswender Str. 10 (Inner Districts) ❶ 167 48 70 ⓦ www.hotel-savoy.de ⓝ U-Bahn: Christuskirche

Agenda 21 Haus ££ One of the most stylish and well-designed hotels in Hanover, with themed rooms. ⓐ Wülferoderstr. 62–72 (City Centre) ❶ 563 580 ⓦ www.agenda21-haus.de ⓝ U-Bahn: Kronsberg

Avalon ££ Nice combination of class and grace. ⓐ Ferdinand-Wallbrecht-Str. 10 (Inner Districts) ❶ 626 263 38 ⓦ www.avalon-hannover.de ⓝ U-Bahn: Lister Platz

City-Hotel Flamme ££ Mediterranean-style *Pension*. a Lammstr. 3 (City Centre) ① 388 80 04 Ⓦ www.city-hotel-flamme.de Ⓝ U-Bahn: Hauptbahnhof

Concorde Am Leineschloss Hotel ££ Old town digs, right in the city centre. Clean, with friendly staff. a Am Markte 12 (City Centre) ① 357 910 Ⓦ www.concorde-hotels.de Ⓝ U-Bahn: Markthalle/Landtag

Crowne Plaza Hanover £££ Luxe to the highest extent; near the main railway station. a Hinüberstr. 6 (City Centre) ① 349 50 Ⓦ www.ichotelsgroup.com Ⓝ Bus 128: Königstrasse

Grand Hotel Mussmann £££ Fabulously maintained treasure near the railway station. Quiet rooms and refined décor. a Ernst-August Pl. 7 (City Centre) ① 365 60 Ⓦ www.grandhotel.de Ⓝ U-Bahn: Hauptbahnhof

Kastens Hotel Luisenhof £££ One of the city's most regal places to rest your head. a Luisenstr. 1–3 (City Centre) ① 304 48 40 Ⓦ www.kastens-luisenhof.de Ⓝ U-Bahn: Kröpcke

Maritim Grand Hotel £££ Hard on the eye outside, more diplomatic inside. Where visiting statesmen stay. a Friedrichswall 11 (City Centre) ① 367 70 Ⓦ www.maritim.de Ⓝ U-Bahn: Aegi

Ramada Hotel Europa £££ Great for those not wanting to stay near the centre or wanting somewhere with lots of business-like extras.

ⓐ Bergstr. 2 (Outer Districts) ❶ 952 80 Ⓦ www.ramada-hotels-hannover.de Ⓝ U-Bahn: Messe/Ost

APARTMENTS

Gästeresidenz PelikanViertel £ Apartment accommodation in a central location. ⓐ Pelikanstr. 11 (City Centre) ❶ 399 90 Ⓦ www.gaesteresidenz-pelikanviertel.de Ⓝ U-Bahn: Pelikanstrasse

Gästehaus an der Schleuse ££ Apartment houses in the Anderten quarter. ⓐ Gollstr. 31 (Outer Districts) ❶ 952 40 84 Ⓦ www.gollhaus.de Ⓝ Bus 125: Anderten Mitte

HOSTELS

Hostel Hannover £ Private hostel. Laundry facilities. ⓐ Lenaustr. 12A (Outer Districts) ❶ 131 99 19 Ⓦ www.hostelhannover.de Ⓝ U-Bahn: Goetheplatz

Jugendherberge Hannover £ Laundry facilities, café/bar, internet access. Wheelchair accessible. ⓐ Ferd.-Wilh.-Fricke-Weg 1 (Outer Districts) ❶ 131 76 74 Ⓦ www.jugendherberge.de/jh/Hannover Ⓝ Bus: 131, 132

CAMPSITE

Erholungsgebiet Blauer See Showers, electricity, cabins. ⓐ Am Blauen See 119, Hannover-Garbsen (Outer Districts) ❶ 0513 789 960 Ⓦ www.camping-blauer-see.de Ⓝ S-Bahn: Waldschenke

THE BEST OF HANOVER

Whether you have some time to kill between business activities, or are visiting Hanover as part of a trip through northern Germany, the following should not be missed.

TOP 10 ATTRACTIONS

- **Neues Rathaus** Offers one of the best views of Hanover in the city. Check out the cool sideways elevator (see page 66)

- **Kröpcke (Clock Square)** It all begins here – casual meetings and subway connections to the city and region (see page 64)

- **Faust in Linden** This former factory now serves as one of Hanover's best entertainment venues (see page 88)

- **Sprengel Museum** World-renowned for its permanent collection and excellent exhibitions (see page 68)

🔻 *Strolling in the Eilenriede*

- **Skulpturenmeile and Nanas** Most famous creations of the American-French artist Niki de Saint Phalle, and works by her well known associates (see page 66)

- **Herrenhäuser Gärten** Four large baroque-style gardens make up this horticulture explosion (see page 77)

- **Marktkirche** Reconstructed after the Allied bombings of World War II (see page 48)

- **Altes Rathaus** Looking more new than old, this is the place where political happenings used to take place (see page 60)

- **Hanover Opera House** The symbol of Hanover; amazing when illuminated at night (see page 22)

- **Eilenriede** A local favourite – Europe's largest city park – and almost twice the size of New York's Central Park (see page 76)

Suggested itineraries

HALF-DAY: HANOVER IN A HURRY

Start at the Neues Rathaus (see page 66). Take the crazy elevator all the way to the top to see nearly to the Hartz Mountains in the west. Cross the road towards the Maritim Grand Hotel, then walk west towards the Altstadt. Look up and to the south for a glimpse of the Waterloo Column (see page 85). See the bronze

⬥ *The burned-out shell of the Aegidienkirche*

figures above the Leine, then glide through the Altstadt for a look at Hanover's oldest buildings. Head in the direction of Clevertor, on the Leine, and appreciate the Nanas and part of the Skulpturenmeile (see page 66). Stop for a Turkish coffee near Steintor. Head north from Steintor to see the Opera House (see page 22), then hop on a tram and head for the Herrenhäuser Gärten (see page 77).

1 DAY: TIME TO SEE A LITTLE MORE

Plug into more of what Hanover has to offer by enjoying the German Impressionist collection or an exhibit at the Sprengel Museum (see page 68). Head to the Maschsee for a quick stroll, then to the Aegidienkirche (see page 60). Take a break at Kröpcke (see page 64) or the Markthalle (see page 70).

2–3 DAYS: TIME TO SEE MUCH MORE

Visit any of the above sights you missed, then head to the Hanover Zoo (see page 77). Picnic or walk through the Eilenriede (see page 76). Make your way to the Jazz Club Hannover (see page 88) or Faust (see page 88), both in Linden.

LONGER: ENJOYING HANOVER TO THE FULL

After a long day's sightseeing around the city, eat dinner at one of the city's many top-notch restaurants. Not being pressed for time means that you can really relax into a day trip. The towns surrounding Hanover showcase some of the quainter tourist options in the region, but especially try to get to Bremen (see page 116) or Celle (see page 104). Peine's Rausch Schokoland (see page 100) is a great place to learn about chocolate, and then eat some.

Something for nothing

Hanover is a reasonably affordable place to visit, except for accommodation if you come during one of the trade fairs. But worry not if the price of your hotel room is enough to sink a small ship: the places listed below offer low budget, high octane ways of seeing and enjoying the city.

One of the lasting impressions of Hanover is the Nanas (see page 66), situated along the Leine river. Created by Niki de Saint Phalle in the 1970s, these colourful feminine figures dance along the river and are illuminated at night. Enjoy the Maschsee lake, and the large festival there in summer. Access to both is free, and places to grab a snack, rest or picnic are never hard to find.

See the red stripe of paint throughout the city centre, the Altstadt and near the Markthalle? Begin at the tourist information centre (see page 137), then follow the red thread until you end up at the Hauptbahnhof. This self-guided tour is free, but an accompanying tourist booklet explaining the historical importance of each site costs about €2.

If you are lucky enough to be in Hanover on a Friday, most of the state-run museums have free admission all day, as does the Kestner (see page 68). The Lower Saxony State Museum (see page 68) is free only from 14.00–17.00 that day.

In the evenings, you can enjoy free classical music concerts twice a season with the 'Classics in the Old Town' events. Held near the Marktkirche (see page 48), they highlight local classical musicians.

Brewery tours are a great, inexpensive way to learn about Hanover's brewery culture. Gilde and Herrenhauser both do guided tours, but by appointment only. Both tours cost around €7, and end with a sample of various beers.

◢ One of the extraordinary, colourful Nanas

When it rains

Hanover's weather pattern can be quite unpredictable, but when the rainy season begins, you are in for a slick version of the city for a while. Enjoy the rain as the locals do by shopping the drizzle away, entertaining yourself with some cultural activities or watching the downpour from a café or restaurant.

While the shops near Kröpcke cover the basics, head to Luisenstrasse, Lister Meile or the hip boutiques in Linden or the Nordstadt for something a bit fancier. **Galerie Luise** (ⓦ www.galerieluise-online.de), on Luisenstrasse, is Hanover's designer destination; a two-storey conglomerate of stores, cafés, banks and speciality boutiques. Across the street, you'll find other designer brands, including a few big French and Italian names. And don't think this part of the *Strasse* (street) is restricted to clothes for those eating solid foods. You'll find a few stores devoted exclusively to clothes for children and babies.

Lister Meile, Linden and the Nordstadt offer similar goods, but focus on different markets. Up and comers head to Lister Meile, hipsters and hippies to Linden and the Nordstadt. The shops on Lindener Marktplatz, Christuskirche and Kopernikusstrasse, and near the U-Bahn stations, should keep you occupied until the precipitation stops.

A rainy day is a good opportunity to catch up on museums, exhibitions and culture. Try the Kestner-Museum (see page 68) for its out of the ordinary and searing political works. Or enjoy a show in the Schauspielhaus (see page 68) or even an English-language movie at the cinema in the **Künstlerhaus** (ⓐ Sophienstr. 2 ⓣ 168 412 22). Or go to the **Marktkirche**

(ⓐ Hanns-Lilje-Platz ❶ 0511 364 370 ⏰ 10.00–18.00) for a tour of the remarkable, Gothic-style edifice. The food stalls in the Markthalle around the corner are a good place to get a quick meal.

The cafés atop Karstadt and Galeria Kaufhof department stores (see page 69) both offer inexpensive lunches and snacks plus decent, dry views of the city when the rain stops.

🔺 *Sculpture outside the Kestner-Museum*

On arrival

TIME DIFFERENCE
Germany uses Central European Time (CET). During Daylight Saving Time (late March–late October), clocks are advanced one hour.

ARRIVING
By air
Located 11 km (7 miles) northwest of the city centre in Lagenhagen, **Hannover-Langenhagen Airport** (HAJ) is served by Lufthansa, Air France, British Airways, Hapag-Lloyd and Turkish Airlines, among others. ❶ 977 12 23 ⓦ www.hannover-airport.de

To get to the Hauptbahnhof (main railway station) via public transport, follow the signs to S-Bahn railway line S5. Journey time from the airport to the Hauptbahnhof is 20 minutes and costs around €2.70 per person for a single trip.

Beige taxis await travellers in various locations outside the arrivals hall and cost approx €25–30 for a trip to the city centre. Be sure to ask in advance what the total cost for a trip to the centre will be. You can pre-book via ⓦ www.flughafen-taxi-hannover.de

By rail
The main railway station – Hannover Hauptbahnhof – lies in the centre of the city. It serves as a connection hub for major Deutsche Bahn routes including non-stop services to Paris and Berlin-Amsterdam (ⓦ www.bahn.de). It is also a connection point for the red and blue ÜSTRA tram lines.

During international trade fairs, some trains from major cities stop at the Hannover Messe/Laatzen station and at the

Messegelände (fair grounds), in the southwest of the city.

Car hire services, travel agents, a grocery store, currency exchanges and ATMs and a trade fair information counter can be found at the Hauptbahnhof, as can a chemist.

The tourist information centre is located directly outside the main entrance and to the left. Look for the Sparda-Bank building: ATMs are also located in here. To the right are the local main offices for Deutsche Post and Postbank.

By road

From the ferry at Calais head for the E15/A216, towards Dunkerque/ Lille. Take the A16, into Belgium, then follow road signs to Antwerpen-Oost, which becomes the E34 as you cross into the Netherlands, and the A67/A40. Then look for signs to Hannover/ Du-Kaiserberg/ Arnheim/Köln, following the A3 then the A2.

Car parks are located throughout the city. The largest ones in the centre are behind the Hauptbahnhof, near Steintor on Kanalstrasse and beneath the opera house.

The minimum age for driving in Germany is 18 and foreign drivers require a valid licence plus proof of insurance. A country identification sticker must be displayed on the vehicle. Traffic drives on the right with speed limits of 130 kph (80 mph) or 100 kph (62 mph) outside built-up areas. Fifty kph (31 mph) is the limit in built-up areas. There are no speed limits on Autobahnen (motorways).

Seatbelts must be worn at all times and children under 12 years can travel in the front seat only with a child restraint.

Don't drink and drive. German laws are strict: the legal maximum alcohol to blood ratio is 0.05 per cent.

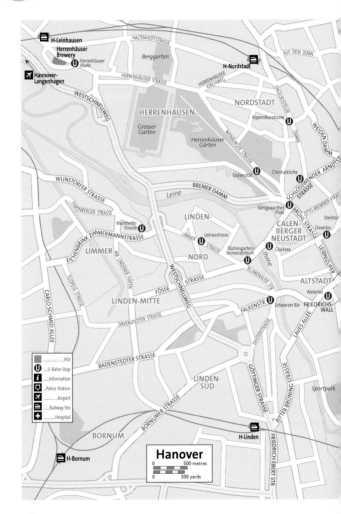

H-Leinhausen

Herrenhäuser Brewery

Herrenhäuser Markt

Hannover-Langenhagen

HALTENHOFFSTRASSE

Berggarten

H-Nordstadt

AUF DEM DORN

HERRENHÄUSER STRASSE

HERRENHÄUSER KIRCHWEG

NORDSTADT

Kopernikusstrasse

WESTSCHNELLWEG

HERRENHAUSEN

Grosser Garten

Herrenhäuser Gärten

Universität

Christuskirche

SCHLOSSWENDER

WEIDEN DAMM

ENGELBOSTELER DAMM

WUNSTORFER STRASSE

BREMER DAMM

Leine

OTTO BRENNER STRASSE

BRÜHL STRASSE

ARNDTSTRASSE

Königsworther Platz

Steintor

HAGENBERGER STRASSE

ZIMMERMANNSTRASSE

LINDEN-

Wunstorfer Strasse

LIMMER STRASSE

Leinaustrasse

Küchengarten/ Immenzentrum

Clevertor

LEIBNIZUFER

Ihme

CALEN BERGER NEUSTADT

EICHENBRINK

LIMMER

NORD

ALTE LINDENER HAFEN

BLUMENAUER STR

Glocksee

Clevertor

CARLO SCHMID ALLEE

SOHRD STRASSE

FÖSSE

WESTSCHNELLWEG

STRASSE

ALTSTADT

Waterloo

Schwarzer Bär

FRIEDRICHS-WALL

FALKENSTR

LINDEN-MITTE

DAVENSTEDTER STRASSE

OESTERSTRASSE

LAVES ALLEE

RITTER BRÜNING STRASSE

	...POI
U	...U-Bahn Stop
i	...Information
⊙	...Police Station
✈	...Airport
🚉	...Railway Stn
✚	...Hospital

BADENSTEDTER STRASSE

LINDEN-SÜD

GÖTTINGER STRASSE

Sportpark

BORNUMER STRASSE

BORNUM

H-Linden

FRIEDRICH EBERT STR

H-Bornum

Hanover

0 — 500 metres

0 — 500 yards

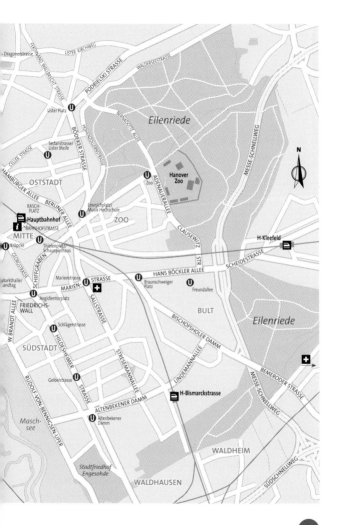

IF YOU GET LOST, TRY ...

Excuse me, do you speak English?
Entschuldigen Sie, sprechen Sie Englisch?
Entshuldigen zee, shprekhen zee english?

Excuse me, is this the right way to the old town/the city centre/the tourist office/the station/the bus station?
Entschuldigung, geht es hier zur Altstadt/zur Stadtmitte/ zur Touristeninformation/zum Bahnhof/zum Busbahnhof?
Entshuldeegoong, gayt es here tsoor altshtat/tsoor shtatmitter/ zur Touristeninformasion/tsoom baanhof/tsoom busbaanhof?

Can you point to it on my map, please?
Können Sie es mir bitte auf der Karte zeigen?
Kernen see es meer bitter owf der kaarte tsygen?

FINDING YOUR FEET

When Hanover was rebuilt after the devastation of the Allied bombings during World War II, it was done so more for function than for aesthetics. So, although Hanover does not have a reputation for being a pretty place, it is very efficient and easy to navigate for visitors. City area maps are posted on the street, and most streets are clearly labelled with buildings following a rational numbering system. Traffic though can be heavy, and disrupted in the city centre due to ongoing construction.

Most areas are safe at night, but visitors should practise common sense at all times, as they would anywhere else. The railway station can be a problem area – but there's a police station on the premises.

ORIENTATION

Hannover Mitte (the centre of town) is decently compact and easily accessible for those with bicycles or the more adventuresome on foot. The Hauptbahnhof plus Bahnhofstrasse and Kröpcke make up the main thoroughfare. Georgstrasse, which extends west to Steintor and east to Aegidientorplatz is also at the heart of the city. Behind the Hauptbahnhof, Hamburger Allee changes into Berliner Allee after the Raschplatz. Marienstrasse east of the train station, on to Friedrichswall, then Leibnizufer and Otto-Brenner-Strasse and Cellerstrasse finish up the ring.

If you find yourself lost, head to the nearest U-Bahn station. Most are equipped with maps of the local area and, if all else fails, all trains intersect at Kröpcke.

GETTING AROUND

ÜSTRA manages Hanover's very organised public transport system, which includes buses, S-Bahn train lines (regional trains operated jointly with Deutsche Bahn and Metronom) and tram lines. The easiest way to get around the town centre in Hanover is by using the efficient electronic tram system. All lines intersect at Kröpcke and run through the Hauptbahnhof or Aegidientorplatz. Tramlines are colour-coded yellow, red or blue. Look for green signs to indicate a bus stop. Information at all stations is listed in German, English and French.

Make sure you validate your ticket on the U-Bahn platform or on the train. If you haven't got a valid ticket, you are fined.

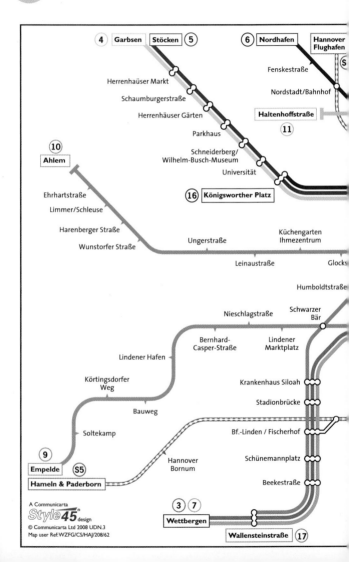

(4) Garbsen | Stöcken (5)   (6) Nordhafen | Hannover Flughafen (S)

Fenskestraße

Herrenhäuser Markt

Nordstadt/Bahnhof

Schaumburgerstraße

Herrenhäuser Gärten   Haltenhoffstraße

(11)

Parkhaus

Schneiderberg/
Wilhelm-Busch-Museum

Universität

(10)
Ahlem   (16) Königsworther Platz

Ehrhartstraße

Limmer/Schleuse

Harenberger Straße   Küchengarten
Ihmezentrum

Wunstorfer Straße   Ungerstraße

Leinaustraße   Glocks

Humboldtstraße

Schwarzer
Bär

Nieschlagstraße

Bernhard-   Lindener
Casper-Straße   Marktplatz

Lindener Hafen

Krankenhaus Siloah

Körtingsdorfer
Weg   Stadionbrücke

Bauweg

Bf.-Linden / Fischerhof

Soltekamp

Schünemannplatz

(9)
Empelde   (S5)   Hannover
Bornum   Beekestraße

Hameln & Paderborn

A Communicarta
Style 45 design
© Communicarta Ltd 2008 UDN.3
Map user Ref:WZFG/CS/HAJ/208/62

(3) (7)
Wettbergen

Wallensteinstraße (17)

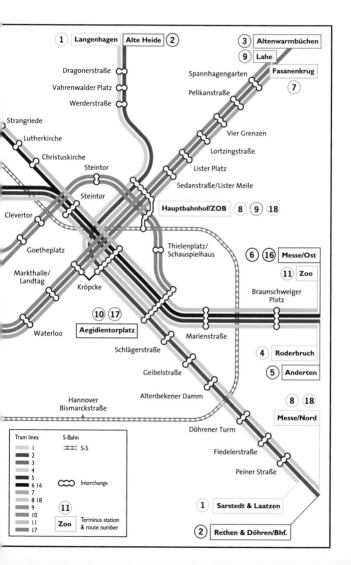

If you are travelling in a group of two or more people, or if you plan on using public transport for more than one ride on your day of arrival, buy an EinzelTagesTicket (around €6.30 for a single-day, three-zone ticket). If your party includes two to five people, buy a TagesGruppenTicket (€12.60 for a single-day, three-zone ticket). The **Hanover Card** (ⓦ www.gvh.de) is a good option for those planning to visit museums and cultural sights.

Taxis are safe and most drivers speak English. There are taxi stands outside the main station, Kröpcke, Steintor and near the Raschplatz.

Transport to the small villages outside the city is usually easiest via S-Bahn. Bremen and Celle are accessed by the R2 and the S3 or R6 respectively. Regional buses are also an option, but these can be quite slow, so opt for the trains if possible.

CAR HIRE

Hanover and the surrounding communities are well connected via public transport, but hiring a car is advisable for those willing to bear the expense. A day rental for a mid-size car excluding petrol and insurance is around €40.

Avis ⓐ Ernst-August Pl. 1 (Hauptbahnhof) ⓣ 322 610
ⓦ www.avis.de

Europcar ⓐ Vahrenwalder Str. 197 ⓣ 355 660 ⓦ www.europcar.de

Hertz ⓐ Schulenburger Landstr. 152 ⓣ 635 092 ⓦ www.hertz.de

Sixt/Budget ⓐ Karl-Wiechert-Allee 74 ⓣ 547 41 41 ⓦ www.sixt.com

◗ *Leibniz House*

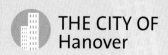

City centre

Hanover has one, single defined centre with other locations of
interest outside it. Many of the city's offerings lie within easy
walking distance of the main railway station and Kröpcke (the
clock tower), or are one stop by public transport from either
starting point; end your journey at either point or in the
Altstadt. Unless otherwise noted, admission is free.

SIGHTS & ATTRACTIONS

Aegidienkirche (Church of St Aegidien)

One of the original city structures, this now burned-out
church was destroyed in 1943. It serves as a local memorial
to victims of violence and war; the Spartans' stone honours
the memory of seven local heroes. ⓐ Breitestr. Ⓝ U-Bahn:
Aegidientorplatz

Altes Rathaus (The Old Town Hall)

Don't mistake this old town hall for the new one. It may look like
it's had a modern facelift, but it was built in the 15th century and
is older than the one near the Maschsee. ⓐ Karmarschstr. 42
ⓘ 300 80 40 Ⓝ U-Bahn: Markthalle/Landtag

Altstadt (The Town Hall)

Come here for a glimpse of what life was like hundreds of years
ago. Although much of the Altstadt was reconstructed after
World War II by collecting old homes throughout the city and
moving them here, you'll understand much about local history

from a walk around. The old city gates are still standing.
🔘 U-Bahn: Markthalle/Landtag

Anzeiger Hochhaus (Anzeiger Skyscraper)

Home to the popular regional newspaper, *Hannoversche Allgemeine Zeitung*, this Expressionist building was completed in 1928. It is the oldest skyscraper in Hanover and one of the few buildings not destroyed in World War II. It is illuminated at night. 🔘 Goseriede 9 🔘 U-Bahn: Steintor

🔺 *Hanover's Expressionist skyscraper – the Anzeiger building*

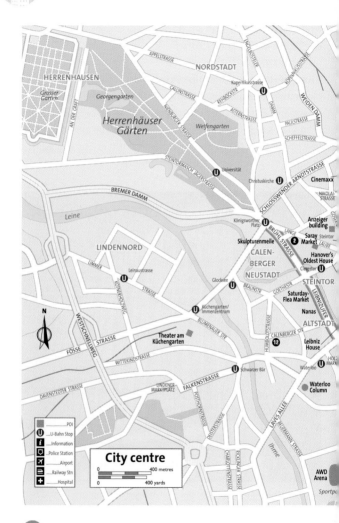

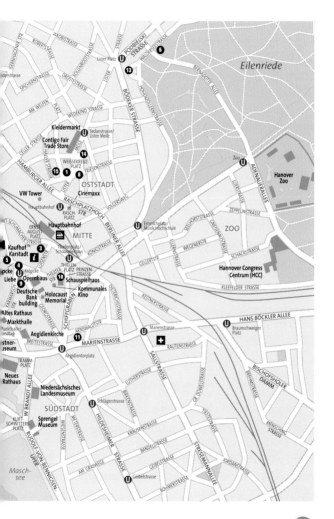

Deutsche Bank building

Built in 1900 under architect Karl Bürgermann, this building was the original site of the Hannover Bank. There are no tours, but its design and history make this location worth a visit.
ⓐ Georgspl. 20 Ⓝ U-Bahn: Kröpcke

Hanover's Oldest House

Parts of this structure date back to the 16th century. Well worth a look, even though you can't get in. In the Altstadt near 'Golden Corner' and the Kreuzkirche (Holy Cross Church).
ⓐ Burgstrasse 12 Ⓝ U-Bahn: Clevertor

Holocaust Memorial

Hanover pays tribute to the 1,882 Jewish citizens who were deported and murdered during the Holocaust. This outdoor memorial, of light-coloured stone, located near the opera house, is engraved with the names, ages and dates of deportation of those murdered. The memorial's designer is the renowned Italian artist Michelangelo Pistoletto (born in 1933). ⓐ Georgstrasse at the intersection with Windmühlenstrasse Ⓝ U-Bahn: Kröpcke

Kröpcke (Clock Square)

Most of the city's festivals, marathons, protests and everyday get-togethers begin here. Come for people-watching and for the several cafés or watering holes. The square and its *Uhr* (clock) are named after Wilhelm Kröpcke, one of the owners of the Café Robby, which later became known as Café Kröpcke. The clock is a 1977 replica of the 1885 original, which was scrapped after World War II. Ⓝ U-Bahn: Kröpcke

● *Holocaust Memorial*

Leibniz House

A replica of the house Leibniz occupied during his time as royal counsellor. The original was destroyed during the Allied bombings of World War II. Holzmarkt 4–6 U-Bahn: Markthalle/Landtag

Lister Meile

As well as one of the shopping meccas, Lister Meile showcases many of the buildings not damaged during World War II. Walk along this *Meile* (mile) of residential and commercial real estate for a peek at some of Hanover's oldest and fanciest homes. U-Bahn: Sedanstrasse/Lister Meile or Lister Platz

Neues Rathaus

Built from 1901–13, this is home to the mayor of Hanover. At 98 m (321 ft) the viewing platform affords one of the best views of Hanover city. Enjoy the crooked elevator. Travelling at a slant and allowing only five people on board at a time, it is well worth queuing for. Also check out the models of the city showing the destruction of Hanover after the Allied bombings. Trammpl. 2 16 80 U-Bahn: Aegidientorplatz

Skulpturenmeile and Nanas

This street art project originated in the 1970s with sculptures from John Henry, Niki de Saint Phalle and Kenneth Snelson, among others. Many of the metal, ceramic and stone creations are illuminated at night. 2km between the Landtag and the Herrenhäuser Gärten. U-Bahn: Clevertor or Königsworther Platz

VW Tower

Next to the ZOB (central bus station). Although once used as a telecommunications tower, nowadays it serves as a full-time billboard for Volkswagen. Also known as Telemoritz, and 141 m (463 ft) high, it was built in 1958. ⓐ Raschplatz-Hochstrasse ⓝ U-Bahn: Hauptbahnhof

🔻 *VW Tower*

CULTURE

Kestner-Museum

Named after the last owner of much of the collection, this museum of applied arts contains ancient Egyptian, Greek and Roman, as well as other art objects. ⓐ Trammpl. 3 ⓣ 168 421 20 ⓦ www.kestner-museum.de ⓛ 11.00–18.00 Tues–Sun, until 20.00 Wed ⓝ U-Bahn: Aegidientorplatz. Admission charge, free Fri

Niedersächsisches Landesmuseum (Lower Saxony State Museum)

Archiving the history of Hanover city and region from prehistoric times to the modern age. ⓐ Willy-Brandt-Allee 5 ⓣ 980 76 86 ⓦ www.landesmuseum-hannover.niedersachsen.de ⓛ 10.00–17.00 Tues–Sun, until 19.00 Thur ⓝ U-Bahn: Aegidientorplatz. Admission charge, free Fri 14.00–17.00

Schauspielhaus

Good selection of stage performances, but mostly in German.

SPRENGEL MUSEUM

One of the most important art museums in Germany, focusing on 20th-century and contemporary art from Germany and all over the world. Niki de Saint Phalle donated over 300 of her works here, on her death. ⓐ Kurt-Schwitters-Pl. 1 ⓣ 168 438 75 ⓦ www.sprengel-museum.de ⓛ 10.00–20.00 Tues, 10.00–18.00 Wed–Sun ⓝ Bus 131/132: Sprengel Museum. Admission charge

---

Check schedule for show times and English-language selections.
ⓐ Prinzenstr. 9 ⓣ 999 911 11 ⓦ www.staatstheater-hannover.de
ⓝ U-Bahn: Thielenplatz/Schauspielhaus

RETAIL THERAPY

Hanover's main shopping area may leave something to be desired, but venture to Lister Meile or Luisenstrasse for more sumptuous and imaginative goods.

Contigo Fair Trade Store Feel good about shopping in this small but colour-drenched shop since all the craftspeople are paid a sustainable wage for their work. Mostly goods from other lands.
ⓐ Lister Meile 29A ⓣ 600 50 30 ⓦ www.contigo-hannover.de
ⓛ 10.00–19.00 Mon–Fri, 10.00–18.00 Sat ⓝ U-Bahn: Lister Meile

Flea Market along Leibnizufer The weekly flea market along the banks of the Leine river is the largest in town. Great for people-watching or shopping. Watch out for pickpockets.
ⓛ 07.00–16.00 Sat ⓝ U-Bahn: Clevertor

Hanover Tourist Information Office Well-priced, quality souvenirs and books about the city and local magazines (in German).
ⓐ Ernst-August-Pl. 8 ⓣ 123 45 11 ⓦ www.hannover.de ⓝ U-Bahn: Hauptbahnhof ⓛ 09.00–18.00 Mon–Fri, 09.00–14.00 Sat

Karstadt and **Galeria Kaufhof** are the city's largest department stores. Both offer similar goods, although Karstadt has a separate sports section. Kaufhof has a second branch near the Altstadt.

Karstadt Georgstr. 23 30 50 09.30–20.00 Mon–Sat U-Bahn: Kröpcke; **Galeria Kaufhof** Ernst-August-Pl. 5 360 10 09.30–20.00 Mon–Sat U-Bahn: Hauptbahnhof

Kleidermarkt *The* location for vintage and used clothing. A national chain of stores selling items by weight, not piece. Check out the military uniforms in the back. Items are 30 per cent cheaper on Wednesdays. Lister Meile 35A 348 17 01 11.00–19.00 Mon–Fri, 11.00–18.00 Sat U-Bahn: Sedanstrasse/Lister Meile

Lister Meile Shop here for a sample of Hanover's home-grown boutiques. Clothing, foodstuffs and shoe stores plus a bit of everything else. U-Bahn: Sedanstrasse/Lister Meile or Lister Platz

Markthalle Twenty-odd stalls sell local and international foodie treats including horsemeat sausages and pickled fish sandwiches. Great for home or a quick lunch. Karmarschstr. 49 07.00–20.00 Mon–Wed, 07.00–22.00 Thur & Fri, 07.00–16.00 Sat U-Bahn: Markthalle/Landtag

Perfumery Liebe Excite your olfactory glands when you enter this indulgent shop, dating back to 1871. Karmarschstr. 25 304 711 www.liebe-hannover.de 09.30–19.00 Mon–Wed & Fri, 09.30–20.00 Thur, 09.00–18.00 Sat U-Bahn: Kröpcke

Saray Market The largest Turkish food market in Hanover. Come here for flat bread, olives, yoghurts and spices. Deli, butcher and household items also sold. Lange Laube 3 167 47 78 08.00–20.00 Mon–Sat U-Bahn: Steintor

TAKING A BREAK

Al Hayat Falafel £ ❶ The best falafel joint in town plus low prices make this a great place to nibble. ⓐ Friesenstr. 58 ⓛ 12.00–02.00 ⓝ U-Bahn: Hauptbahnhof

Café Caldo £ ❷ Known as a hotspot for Hanover's gay community, this place is more bar than café. Great drink specials and a good location entice you to stay on into the late evening. ⓐ Bergmannstr. 7, off Lange Laube ⓣ 151 73 ⓦ www.caldo.de ⓛ 18.00–late Mon–Fri & Sun, 20.00–late Sat ⓝ U-Bahn: Steintor

Eiscafe Bistro Coliseum £ ❸ Generously proportioned sandwiches, coffees and, of course, ice cream are on offer here. If the weather's clement, there's a massive outdoor seating area. ⓐ Ernst-August-Pl. 1 ⓣ 306 91 11 ⓛ 05.00–02.00 ⓝ U-Bahn: Hauptbahnhof

Giovanni L. Eiscafe £ ❹ One of Hanover's favourite places to hang out. Amazing ice cream selection. ⓐ Georgstr. 23 ⓛ 10.30–22.30 Mon–Sat ⓝ U-Bahn: Kröpcke

Karstadt Panorama Restaurant £ ❺ As the name suggests, wonderful views of the city and great for people-watching and to relax after a long day of sightseeing. There's a child-friendly seating area. ⓐ Georgstr. 23 ⓣ 305 23 05 ⓛ 08.45–20.00 Mon–Sat ⓝ U-Bahn: Kröpcke

Lister Turm Biergarten £ ❻ Over 400 places to sit and enjoy a beer in this large beer garden near the Eilenriede (see page 76).

ⓐ Walderseestr. 100 ⓣ 696 56 03 ⓦ www.lister-turm-biergarten-hannover.de ⓛ 12.00–00.00, summer only
ⓝ U-Bahn: Lister Platz

Atrium in the Altes Rathaus ££ ❼ Come here for afternoon tea or Sunday brunch. Near the Maschsee lake. Casual but stylish.
ⓐ Karmarschstr. 42 ⓣ 300 80 40 ⓛ 12.00–14.30, 16.00–00.00 Mon–Sat ⓝ Bus 120, 131, 132: Rathaus

Café Mezzo ££ ❽ Where else can you touch all four corners of the culinary world plus hang out with the art crowd and students? Part of Pavillon (see page 74). ⓐ Lister Meile 4
ⓣ 314 966 ⓦ www.cafe-mezzo.de ⓛ 09.00–02.00 Sun–Thur, 09.00–03.00 Fri & Sat ⓝ U-Bahn: Hauptbahnhof

enercity expo Café ££ ❾ Admire the lustrous purple and fuchsia décor while you enjoy lunch and café food – soups, sandwiches and pasta. ⓐ Ständehausstr. 6, off Karmarschstr. ⓣ 326 284 59
ⓦ www.enercity.de ⓛ 10.00–23.00 ⓝ U-Bahn: Kröpcke

AFTER DARK

RESTAURANTS
heimW £ ❿ One chilled place to lounge around. Cool leather furniture, inspired light fittings and a massive fish tank. Keep walking to the back if you can't find a place to sit in front. ⓐ Theaterstr. 6 ⓣ 235 23 03 ⓦ www.heim-w.de
ⓛ 09.00–01.00 Mon–Thur, 09.00–02.00 Fri & Sat, 10.00–01.00 Sun ⓝ U-Bahn: Kröpcke

da Lello ££ ⓫ Outstanding wine selection and knowledgeable staff. Try the seafood at this Italian restaurant. It may not look it from the outside, but it's popular with Hanover's upper crust. ⓐ Marienstr. 5 ⓣ 320 07 05 ⓦ www.dalello.de ⓛ 12.00–15.00, 18.00–00.00 Mon–Sat ⓝ U-Bahn: Aegidientorplatz

Pfannkuchen Haus ££ ⓬ This seemingly ordinary venue is a Hanover institution. There are more than 30 different pancake fillings on offer, both savoury and sweet. If you're not keen on pancakes, try the steak. Also notable is the special set of scales used to weigh the beer. ⓐ Calenberger Str. 27 ⓣ 171 13 ⓦ www.pfannkuchenhaus.de ⓛ 18.00–00.00 Mon–Fri, 12.00–15.00 Sun & holidays ⓝ Bus 120: Calenberger Strasse

Restaurant Kartoffelhaus Hannover ££ ⓭ Potatoes (from a local grower) everywhere, especially on the menu. Enjoy a glass of sweet potato liquor or the recommended fisherman's pan. ⓐ Oskar-Winter-Str. 8, off Hohenzollernstr. ⓣ 660 297 ⓦ www.kartoffelhaus-hannover.de ⓛ 12.00–23.00 Mon–Sat, 12.00–22.00 Sun ⓝ U-Bahn: Lister Platz

Restaurant Clichy £££ ⓮ One of several restaurants owned by local celebrity restaurateur Ekkehard Reimann. French menu focusing on seasonal dishes. ⓐ Weissekreuzstr. 31, off Weissekreuzpl. ⓣ 312 447 ⓦ www.clichy.de ⓛ 12.00–14.30 Mon–Fri, 18.00–23.00 Mon–Sat ⓝ U-Bahn: Sedanstrasse/Lister Meile

Ristorante Del Core £££ ⓯ You can enjoy food from all over Italy when you dine at this authentic restaurant. Sophisticated, but

unpretentious. Reservations advisable, especially on weekends.
Haller Str. 34 519 67 48 12.00–15.00, 18.00–00.00
Bus 128: Celler Strasse

BARS, CLUBS & STEINTOR

Brothels at Steintor Prostitution is legal in Germany. Sex workers
are licensed and have rights. The main area of the sex industry
in Hanover lies on three streets between the main shopping
district and the Altstadt – red light-infused Steintor. Brothels,
sex clubs, bars and strip clubs line the streets, and women are
not allowed to walk in this area at night. After sundown,
year-round including holidays U-Bahn: Steintor

Monsieur Melody Mostly LGBT clientele and a good place
for a casual drink. Friesenstr. 67 318 689 19.00–late
U-Bahn: Hauptbahnhof

Naoum's If you love R 'n' B, reggae, rap, house, latin or Turkish
pop music, this is the place to go dancing when the sun sets.
International acts occasionally up the entertainment ante.
Königstr. 12 0513 063 69 www.naoums-club.de
22.00–late Thur–Sun, but varies according to event
Bus 128: Königstrasse. Admission charge

Pavillon Nice venue focusing on international music, cabaret
and entertainment: Turkish piano players, Polish pop acts and
American gospel singers. Eat at Café Mezzo (see page 72).
Lister Meile 4 235 55 50 Varies www.Pavillon-hannover.de
U-Bahn: Hauptbahnhof

Rockhouse Rock Music location near C&A department store. Good place to hear local bands and booze with those who favour leather jackets and jeans to suits and swank. ⓐ Kurt-Schumacher-Str. 23 ① 165 00 11 ⓦ www.rockhouse-hannover.de ① 22.00–04.00 Wed & Sat, 21.00–04.00 Fri ⓝ U-Bahn: Steintor. Admission charge

ZaZa House music dominates in this uber-cool juke joint near the main railway station. Hanover's high rollers and cool cats come late, and so should you. ⓐ Hamburger Allee 4A ① 314 473 ⓦ www.zaza-club.de ① 22.00–late Thur–Sun ⓝ U-Bahn: Hauptbahnhof. Admission charge

ALTERNATIVES TO BARS & CLUBS

Cinemaxx One of the largest movie chains in Germany. Watch the latest Hollywood blockbuster dubbed in German, rather than wait for the English original to show at a theatre near you. Two cinemas to choose from: ⓐ Rashpl. 6 ⓝ U-Bahn: Hauptbahnhof; ⓐ Nikolaistr. 8 ⓝ Bus: Am Klagesmarkt; ① 01805 246 362 99 ⓦ www.cinnemaxx.de

Kommunales Kino Art house and big budget films. Most are shown in their original language, noted by 'Originalsprache' on the programme, sometimes with German subtitles. ⓐ Sophienstr. 2 ① 168 447 32 ⓦ www.koki-hannover.de ⓝ U-Bahn: Kröpcke

Maschsee The shores of this lake are a safe place for a late-night stroll after dinner or for a day of sightseeing. Pleasing during the day, illuminated at night. ⓝ Bus 131/132: Sprengel Museum

Linden, the Nordstadt & other inner districts

What the centre lacks in spirited, laid-back, chilled-out amusing stuff to see and do, Linden, the Nordstadt and the other inner districts make up for. Linden and the Nordstadt are student and immigrant dominated areas – both lively and more diverse than the centre. Linden, a former town in its own right, offers a good mix of non-generic places to shop and eat. The same can be said for the Zoo and List areas, although they are more expensive. Here, too, you'll find good, low-priced Lebanese, Russian, Turkish, German and Spanish restaurants.

SIGHTS & ATTRACTIONS

Eilenriede
The largest green area in the city – and in Europe – this city park is almost twice the size of New York City's Central Park. In the north is Hanover Zoo and a bird sanctuary. Plus there's a beer garden, myriad footpaths and several monuments. Ⓝ U-Bahn: Hannover Congress Centrum or Zoo

Hannover Congress Centrum (HCC)
Great for sightseeing – the building is worth a look – as well as events: look for the posters listing HCC happenings. Parties for the over-30 crowd, concerts and career fairs have all had their time here. Adjacent to the Eilenriede. ⓐ Theodor-Heuss-Pl. 1–3 ❶ 811 30 ⓦ www.hcc.de Ⓝ U-Bahn: Hannover Congress Centrum

Herrenhäuser Brewery

View production at one of Hanover's only remaining breweries. Tours, available by appointment only, end with a sample of beer. ⓐ Herrenhäuser Str. 83–99 ⓣ 0511 790 70 ⓦ www.herrenhaeuser.de ⓝ U-Bahn: Herrenhäuser Markt. Admission charge

Herrenhäuser Gärten

Step into the world of Hanover's royal gardens, made up of four separate gardens – the French-style baroque Grosser Garten; the English-landscaped Georgengarten; Berggarten and Welfengarten. ⓐ Herrenhäuser Str. 4 ⓣ 168 445 43 ⓦ www.herrenhaeuser-gaerten.de ⓒ 09.00–20.00 summer; 09.00–16.00 winter ⓝ U-Bahn: Herrenhäuser Gärten. Admission charge for Grosser Garten only

Jüdische Gemeinde, Hannover (includes Synagogue)

This is a cemetery, synagogue and community meeting space.

HANOVER ZOO

Originally opened in 1865, this is one of the best zoos in Germany. Don't confuse it though with the Tiergarten in the eastern part of the city (see page 102). Twenty-two hectares (54 acres) are given over to 240 species of animals. ⓐ Adenauerallee 3 ⓣ 280 741 63 ⓦ www.zoo-hannover.de ⓒ 09.00–18.00 summer; 10.00–16.00 winter ⓝ U-Bahn: Zoo. Admission charge

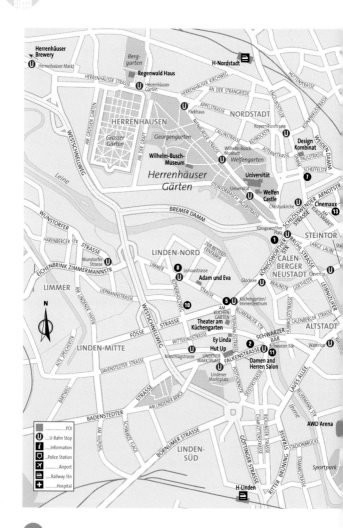

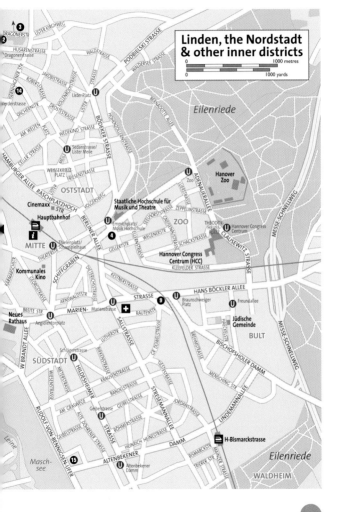

🅐 Haeckelstr. 10 ☎ 810 472 🌐 www.jg-hannover.de
🕐 By appointment only Ⓝ U-Bahn: Freundallee

Leine and Ihme rivers

Begin at U-Bahn station Glocksee or Schwarzer Bär, and walk down to the river. The Leine and Ihme rivers intersect at many points, are generally safe during the day, and are good for walking and biking, rollerblading and frisbee throwing. For a picnic, head for entry near Krankenhaus Siloah.

Welfen Castle

Former winter castle of King George V, completed in 1866 and rebuilt 1875–9 as the seat of the University, with the *Sachsenross* or horse statue in front. 🅐 Am Welfengarten 1 Ⓝ U-Bahn: Universität

◆ *Wilhelm-Busch-Museum*

Wilhelm-Busch-Museum

In the Georgengarten, home to illustrations, caricatures, satirical, political and comic cartoons from the 19th century to the present. The only one of its kind in Germany. Some multimedia exhibits.

ⓐ Georgengarten ❶ 169 999 11 ⓦ www.wilhelm-busch-museum.de ⏰ 11.00–17.00 Tues–Fri, 11.00–18.00 Sat, Sun & holidays Ⓝ U-Bahn: Wilhelm-Busch-Museum. Admission charge

CULTURE

Theater am Küchengarten

TAK offers something traditional in nature, but modern in expression. Comedy and cabaret acts abound, but shows in

English are uncommon. *Kabarettfestival* in early September.
 Am Küchengarten 3–5 445 562 www.tak-hannover.de
 13.00–18.00 Mon–Sat U-Bahn: Küchengarten/
Immenzentrum

RETAIL THERAPY

Adam und Eva Sells many of the fun, young labels from the
UK and the USA. Limmerstr. 45 261 72 80 11.00–19.00
Mon–Fri, 11.00–16.00 Sat U-Bahn: Leinaustrasse

Am Klagesmarkt Come here on Thursdays and Saturdays for
fresh local produce and foodstuffs, some of which are organic.
 07.00–13.00 Thur & Sat U-Bahn: Christuskirche

Damen and Herren Salon Boutique shopping at its
most stylish: this clothing boutique masquerades as
a hairdresser's shop, and has the washbasins to prove it.
 Lindener Marktpl. 12 473 999 91 www.damen-
und-herren-salon.de 11.00–14.00, 15.00–19.00 Mon–Fri,
11.00–14.00 Sat U-Bahn: Lindener Marktplatz

Design Kombinat More young urban hipster and surfer cool
than anywhere else in town. Engelbosteler Damm/Ecke
Paulstr. 1A 763 54 45 www.design-kombinat.com
 11.00–19.00 Mon–Fri, 11.00–16.00 Sat U-Bahn:
Kopernikusstrasse

◗ *Rearing up outside the University – the* Sachsenross

Ey Linda Local and national clothing – more city farm girl chic than edgy urbanite – plus home furnishing designers. Two locations. Stephanusstr. 17 920 86 55 www.eylinda.de 11.00–14.00, 15.00–18.30 Mon–Fri, 11.00–14.00 Sat U-Bahn: Lindener Marktplatz; Lister Meile 31 11.00–19.00 Mon–Fri, 11.00–16.00 Sat U-Bahn: Lister Platz

Hut-Up Beautiful ladies' hats, scarves and purses. Lindener Marktpl. 5 455 796 www.hut-up.de 10.00–18.00 Mon–Fri, 10.00–13.00 Sat U-Bahn: Lindener Marktplatz

Lindener Marktplatz Saturday open-air market for food and other goods, including incense and organic *Essen* (food). 07.00–13.00 Sat U-Bahn: Lindener Marktplatz

TAKING A BREAK

DerMuffinMann £ ❶ This bakery/café serves up enormous muffins: try the classic blueberry or lemon, or other freshly baked varieties of muffins, bagels, cookies and the like. Friendly staff. More seating at Rehbockstrasse. Rehbockstr. 2 123 47 91 www.dermuffinmann.de 08.30–18.00 Mon–Fri, 09.00–14.00 Sat U-Bahn: Kopernikusstrasse; Königswortherstr. 4 U-Bahn: Königsworther Platz

Konditorei und Cafe Mönikes Schwarzer Bär £ ❷ Join Karsten Peters, the master confectioner, at one of the best bakery/cafés in the city. The three-layer chocolate cake is to die for. Falkenstr. 13 454 643 www.hannovers-tortenkoenig.de 07.30–18.00

Mon–Fri, 10.30–18.00 Sun & public holidays ⓝ U-Bahn: Schwarzer Bär

Pâtisserie Elysée £ ❸ Traditional French bakery with a few spaces to sit down and eat. ⓐ Vahrenheider Markt 1 ❶ 374 91 76 ⓦ www.patisserie-elysee.de ⓛ 07.00–18.00 Mon–Fri, 07.30–13.00 Sat, 08.30–17.00 Sun ⓝ S-Bahn: Vahrenheider Markt

Tiffany's £ ❹ Hidden gem not far from the Zoo. Great for lunch or a snack; the pizza is inexpensive and excellent. ⓐ Schiffgraben 48 ❶ 282 461 ⓛ 11.00–00.00 Mon–Sat, 11.00–20.00 Sun ⓝ U-Bahn: Emmichplatz/Musik Hochschule

Waschweiber £ ❺ Whoever thought of doing the weekly wash in a bar? This hip concept bar and coffee house doubles as a launderette, with beer, mixed drinks, cocktails and light snacks on the menu. Popular even if you don't have a load of washing to do. Remember, *Frauen* (women) wash and *Herren* (men) dry: the washing machines are named after women, the dryers after men. Not the cheapest place to do laundry, but undoubtedly the most stimulating and fun. ⓐ Limmerstr. 1 ❶ 123 76 96 ⓛ 11.00–21.00 Mon–Fri, 09.00–21.00 Sat; bar always open until 01.00 ⓝ U-Bahn: Küchengarten/Immenzentrum

Waterloo Biergarten £ ❻ Massive beer garden near the AWD Arena and its namesake, the Waterloo Column. Drink and eat at moderate prices. ⓐ Waterloostr. 1 ❶ 156 43 ⓦ www.waterloo-biergarten.de ⓛ 12.00–00.00 ⓝ U-Bahn: Waterloo

AFTER DARK

RESTAURANTS

Kebap 44 £ ❼ This is one of the best Turkish *Schnellimbiss* (takeaway) bars in town. Two locations on Engelbosteler Damm. There's a stone, wood-fired oven, excellent kebabs and fresh items in the deli counter. ⓐ Engelbosteler Damm 10 and 48 ❶ 701 931 🕐 11.00–00.00 Ⓝ U-Bahn: Christuskirche

Notre Dame £ ❽ Sit outside in good weather if cigarette smoke bothers you, because this place can get smoky. Mostly Italian-inspired pasta dishes, but *Currywurst* is also on the menu in case you need the jolt of German *Imbiss*. Good beer selection and a few good cakes, too. ⓐ Offensteinstr. 1, off Kötnerholzweg ❶ 215 25 06 🕐 09.00–01.00 Mon–Fri, 09.00–02.00 Sat, 08.00–00.00 Sun Ⓝ U-Bahn: Leinaustrasse

Le Monde Bistro ££ ❾ Lovely classic French bistro just outside the Mitte district. Amazingly rich desserts, and snails on the menu. The garden is enjoyable in the summer. ⓐ Marienstr. 116 ❶ 856 51 71 🕐 18.00–00.00 Ⓝ U-Bahn: Braunschweiger Platz

O' Atlantico ££ ❿ A gem of a place to eat. Wooden tables, tiles and flavours all authentic to that land to the south called Spain. Lots of beef on the menu and, as you'd expect, great paella. ⓐ Kötnerholzweg 6 ❶ 448 239 ⓦ www.spanische-restaurants.com 🕐 Food: 18.00–00.00, bar: 18.00–02.00 Ⓝ U-Bahn: Leinaustrasse

Tandure ££ ⓫ On the edge of Linden, this is one of the best Middle-Eastern-style restaurants in Hanover, and one of the few places in town to find hummus on the menu, plus wood-fired oven bakes. Belly dancers Thursday–Saturday. On the Ihme river; take the stairs down by the Irish Harp. ⓐ Deisterstr. 17D ⓣ 453 670 ⓦ www.tandure-restaurant.de ⓛ 12.00–01.00 Wed–Mon ⓝ U-Bahn: Schwarzer Bär

Basil £££ ⓬ In one of 13 buildings in the former grounds of a Prussian riding stable, one of the most popular restaurants in town and one of the tastiest – for Pacific Rim, Eurasian and various European cuisines. A must, if you can afford it. ⓐ Dragonerstr. 30A ⓣ 622 636 ⓦ www.basil.de ⓛ 18.00–02.00 ⓝ U-Bahn: Dragonerstrasse

Gattopardo £££ ⓭ Located just outside the centre, next to the Accor Mitte hotel, and walkable from Steintor. Very creative menu, but has its roots in the Italian kitchen. ⓐ Hainhölzer Str. 1, off Arndtstr. ⓣ 143 75 ⓦ www.gattopardo-hannover.de ⓛ 18.00–00.00 Mon–Sat ⓝ U-Bahn: Steintor; Bus 128: Am Klagesmarkt

Le Chalet £££ ⓮ Classic French restaurant with a distinguished wine selection. Charming ambience and first-class service. ⓐ Isernhagener Str. 21 ⓣ 727 84 15 ⓦ www.lechalet-restaurant.de ⓛ 19.30–23.00 Tues–Sun ⓝ U-Bahn: Werderstrasse

Pier 51 £££ ⓯ One of Hanover's best restaurants, located on the banks of the Maschsee. Intertwining global influences make

this splurge well worth it. ⓐ Rudolf-von-Bennigsen-Ufer 51
ⓣ 807 18 00 ⓦ www.pier51.de ⓛ 12.00–00.00 ⓝ U-Bahn:
Altenbekener Damm

BARS & CLUBS

Bei Chéz Heinz Alternative clubbing and dancing. Music
changes every night, including funk, soul, rock, Brit pop and
house. Cover charge sometimes, but often includes a beer
or other drink from the bar. ⓐ Liepmannstr. 7B ⓣ 214 299 20
ⓦ www.beichezheinz.de ⓛ Varies ⓝ U-Bahn: Wunstorfer Strasse

Bronco's Uber-cool hipster hang-out. Small bi-level bar/lounge
popular with the young hip crowd in Linden. The cocktails are
okay, but stick with beer if you don't like surprises. ⓐ Schwarzer
Bär 7 ⓣ 260 74 53 ⓛ 20.00–late ⓝ U-Bahn: Schwarzer Bär

Faust in Linden This old bed factory in Linden is one of the
biggest and hippest places to enjoy a drink, a light meal or
watch a band play. This cultural powerhouse packs a punch with
a club, bar, two cafés, music stage and other venues – all in one
complex. A bit hard to find, but follow the music to the end of
the street, turn the corner and along the footpath to the main
entrance. Outdoor events in spring. ⓐ Zur Bettfedernfabrik 3
ⓦ www.faustev.de ⓛ 20.00–00.00 Mon–Thur & Sun, 22.00–01.00
Fri, 20.00–02.00 Sat ⓣ 455 001 ⓝ U-Bahn: Leinaustrasse

Jazz Club Hannover Incredible place to hear live jazz, but it can
get smoky. Some of the biggest names in the German jazz scene
play here, as do top international acts. Look out for Swinging

Hannover events in spring and JazzSeminar events year round. The Jazz Museum is also worth a visit. ⓐ Am Lindener Berge 38 ⓣ 454 455 ⓦ www.jazz-club.de ⓛ Varies ⓝ U-Bahn: Nieschlagstrasse; Bus 100 & 200: Sternwarte

Kulturpalast Linden Another chill-out location in Linden, with a mixed crowd of students, urban cat daddies and the relaxed crowd hard to find in the city centre. Trendy interior design, a DJ and sometimes live music events. ⓐ Deisterstr. 24 ⓣ 262 97 33 ⓦ www.kulturpalast-linden.de ⓛ 20.00–late Tues–Sat ⓝ U-Bahn: Schwarzer Bär

Spandau Projekt Don't come for the food (lacklustre and a bit pricey), come for the crowd – and the drinks are a good buy. This lounge acts as a café, coffee bar, bar, entertainment venue and art gallery. Beautiful interior design; in summer, sit upstairs on the rooftop terrace. ⓐ Engelbosteler Damm 30 ⓣ 123 570 95 ⓦ www.spandau-projekt.de ⓛ 10.00–01.00 Sun & Mon, 10.00–02.00 Tues–Sat ⓝ Bus 131/132: Engelbosteler Damm

CINEMA
Apollo Kino für Filmkunst One of the oldest continually operating cinemas in Germany, dating back to 1908. Not only films (normally shown in their original language), but also programmes about films and film making. ⓐ Limmerstr. 50 ⓣ 452 438 ⓦ www.apollokino.de ⓝ U-Bahn: Leinaustrasse

Outer districts & around

Hanover is more than just a city, it's a region, and just a step or two off the normal tourist route are the outer districts and smaller villages, outside of the city centre, which lay claim to some of the most intriguing sights in all of Germany. Although some of these may take you a bit longer to get to, they are all well connected via regional and national trains or by local public transport (buses and trams).

SIGHTS & ATTRACTIONS

WEST OF HANOVER
Observation Deck at Hanover International Airport
A great place to take children, or to relax before your flight home, or if you've visited everything else on your list. Great views of take offs and landings, as well as historical information about the airport. Small gifts available from the kiosk and on-site café by Mövenpick. ⓐ Hannover-Langenhagen Airport ⓦ www.hannover-airport.de ⓛ 12.00–18.00 ⓝ S-Bahn: Hannover Airport. Admission charge

Steinhuder Meer (Steinhude)
If you like outdoor activities such as camping, sailing, fishing, parasailing, biking, horse riding or sunbathing, this is your kind of place. It's very popular with locals for day tripping or weekending. This natural park is surrounded by several small villages, making it a great place to stay for the weekend if you have time and the weather is nice. Although better accessed by car, public transport

is available. Check out the golf courses in the surrounding areas as well, if golf is your sport. ⓝ DB Train: Wunstorf-Steinhude, Bus 710 to the Meer

There are a couple of interesting museums here too: **Das Fischer- und Webermuseum** (Fishing Museum ⓐ Neuer Winkel 8, Wunstorf Steinhude ⓣ 05033 55 99) and **Spielzeugmuseum** (Toy Museum ⓐ Im Scheunenviertel, Steinhude ⓣ 05033 55 99 ⓦ www.steinhuder-museen.de).

Also worth a visit is Europe's largest butterfly farm and insectarium, the **Schmetterlingsfarm Steinhude** (ⓐ Am Knick 5, Steinhude/Steinhuder Meer ⓣ 05033 939 451 ⓦ www.schmetterlingsfarm.de).

Be sure to try some of the smoked fish and eel dishes in local restaurants; much of it is caught fresh in the Meer and smoked on site. Try **Schweer's Fischerei und Aalräucheri** (ⓐ Alter Winkel 6, Wunstdorf/Steinhude ⓣ 05033 84 67 ⓦ www.schweers-fischerei.de) or **Hodann Fisherei** (ⓐ Alter Winkel 1, Wunstdorf/Steinhude ⓣ 05033 82 46).

Provincial boutique shopping is also on offer at the Steinhuder Meer. Try **Leine-Café Heydenreich** (ⓐ Mittelstr. 13, Neustadt a. Rbge ⓣ 05032 801 16 61 ⓦ www.modeproduktion.de). For more information on the area visit **Steinhuder Meer Tourism** (ⓐ Meerstr. 2 ⓣ 05033 950 10 ⓦ www.steinhuder-meer.de).

SOUTH OF HANOVER
Deutsche Messe

The trade fair grounds – Messegelände. As well as being home to CeBIT and other industrial fairs, this is the place to check out some of the city's best architecture. The pavilions from EXPO 2000

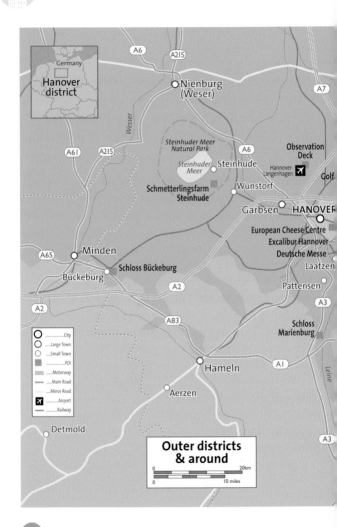

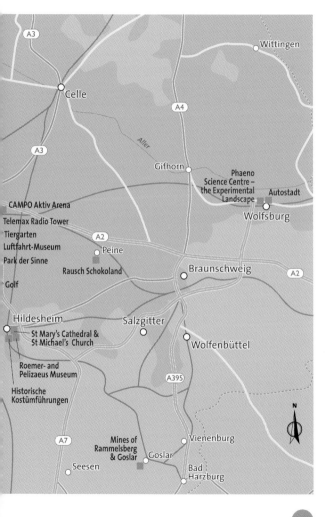

Wittingen

Celle

A3

A4

A3

Aller

Gifhorn

Phaeno
Science Centre –
the Experimental
Landscape
Autostadt

Wolfsburg

CAMPO Aktiv Arena

Telemax Radio Tower

Tiergarten

Luftfahrt-Museum

A2

Peine

Park der Sinne

Rausch Schokoland

Braunschweig

A2

Golf

Hildesheim

Salzgitter

St Mary's Cathedral &
St Michael's Church

Wolfenbüttel

Roemer- and
Pelizaeus Museum

A395

Historische
Kostümführungen

N

A7

Mines of
Rammelsberg
& Goslar

Vienenburg

Goslar

Seesen

Bad
Harzburg

are still standing, many a unique expression of the cultures of the countries concerned. Look for the six-storey post box, one of the world's largest. ⓐ Messegelände ⓣ 890 ⓦ www.hannovermesse.de Ⓝ U-Bahn: Messe/Ost, Messe/Nord; S-Bahn: R10, R11

A Terrific Weekend Expo and **The NDR 2 Plaza Festival** These annual events at the Messe are your chance to kick off the summer entertainment season properly. Live local music acts and local announcers amuse crowds of over 100,000. Usually in early to mid-June. ⓐ Deutsche Messe EXPO Plaza, EXPO-Areal ⓣ 364 380. Admission charge

Historische Kostümführungen, Hildesheim
Learn about the history of Hildesheim and the region through the costumes and entertainment provided by this 'living museum'. Local actors dress in period costumes and lead guided tours of the important sights. Major local personalities are represented on the tour. ⓐ Rathausstr. 18–20 ⓣ 0512 117 980 ⓦ www.costume-event.de ⓛ Tour times vary, check website for details Ⓝ S-Bahn: Hildesheim. Admission charge

CLUBBING AT THE DEUTSCHE MESSE
If you happen to be in town for one of Hanover's many trade fairs, or want something a bit more international, keep your eyes peeled for a night of dancing and drinking at the Deutsche Messe. Various pavilions turn into dance clubs when major fairs are on, so take advantage.

Luftfahrt-Museum (Aviation Museum), Laatzen

Over 4,000 exhibits are on display, ranging from Lilienthal's gliders to Charles Lindbergh's Atlantic crossing to the fighter aircraft of World War II, this place has a bit of everything. Opened in 1992, it is located near the Hannover Trade Fair Center in Laatzen. ⓐ Ulmer Str. 2 ❶ 879 17 91 ⓦ www.luftfahrtmuseum-hannover.de ❶ 10.00–17.00 Tues–Sun Ⓝ U-Bahn: Messe Nord. Admission charge

Park der Sinne (Park of the Senses), Laatzen

A series of gardens and green spaces designed to stimulate your senses. The garden of fragrances appeals to your nose and the echo garden to your ears. Excellent for those with children, or for visitors staying close to the Messe. Designed by landscape architect Hans-Joachim Adam. Exit the tram and head for the main entrance. ⓐ Am Holze ❶ 820 53 43 ⓦ www.laatzen.de Ⓝ U-Bahn: Park der Sinne

Roemer- and Pelizaeus Museum, Hildesheim

World-renowned museum of Egyptian and Peruvian artefacts plus Imperial Chinese porcelain and Asian art. ⓐ Am Steine 1–2 ❶ 0512 193 690 ⓦ www.rpmuseum.de ❶ 10.00–18.00 Tue–Sun Ⓝ S-Bahn: Hildesheim

St Mary's Cathedral and St Michael's Church, Hildesheim

Famed the world over for their ecclesiastical architecture, two neighbouring churches make up this one UNESCO World Heritage Site. St Mary's Cathedral is famous for its artistic treasures and medieval art. Built between 1010 and 1022 by Bishop Bernward,

🔺 *A tranquil spot in the Park der Sinne*

St Michael's Church remains a prime example of Ottonian Romanesque architecture. Be sure to admire the wooden ceiling, the bronze doors and the Bernward bronze column. Also worth a look is the 1,000-year-old rosebush. 🌐 www.welterbe-hildesheim.de 🕐 08.00–18.00 summer; 09.00–16.00 winter Ⓢ S-Bahn: Hildesheim

Schloss Bückeburg (Bückeburg Castle)
Another ode to the royal history of Lower Saxony. This castle is the former home of Prince Ernst von Holstein-Schaumburg – and what a home it is: the magnificent opulence, draped in

regal grandeur, is simply breathtaking. Be sure to visit the Grosser Festsaal and Mausoleum. The rose garden is nice for a stroll. ⓐ Schlosspl. 1, Bückeburg ⓣ 05722 50 39 ⓦ www.schloss-bueceburg.de ⓛ 09.30–18.00 Apr–Sept, 09.30–17.00 Oct–Mar, last admission one hour before closing ⓝ S-Bahn: Bückeburg. Admission charge

Schloss Marienburg (Marienburg Castle)

Happily opened to the public, this castle (the current residence of the remaining Hanover royal family) is a gem for anyone interested in Hanover's regal past. Originally a gift from George V to Queen Marie, the castle is neo-Gothic in shape, but not in structure. It was built between 1857 and 1867, but was never completed because the Prussian annexation of the kingdom in 1866 halted further construction. Former Queen Marie occupied the castle before joining her husband in exile. The former royal family did not return until after the end of World War II. ⓐ Marienburg 1, Pattensen ⓣ 05069 407 ⓦ www.schloss-marienburg.de ⓛ 10.00–18.00 Apr–Nov ⓝ S-Bahn: Pattensen. Admission charge

EAST OF HANOVER
Autostadt, Wolfsburg

You may well have heard about this one – now it's time to visit and see for yourself. Opened in the only city in Germany established for the manufacture of Volkswagen cars, this is one of the snazzier attractions for visitors in the region. It's great for automobile lovers, or simply those in love with the Volkswagen brand. Plan a whole day for a trip out if you want to enjoy all this place has to offer. There are boat rides on the canal, a museum, and countless exhibitions about cars and the VW brand. The food court features some of the best eateries in Wolfsburg. Special offers combine train and admission fares. ⓐ Directly behind Wolfsburg railway station ⓣ 800 288 678 238 ⓦ www.autostadt.de ⓛ 09.00–20.00 ⓝ Trains: direct connections via regional train, but spend the extra money and take the IC or ICE trains – they are much faster. Admission charge

Phaeno Science Centre – the Experimental Landscape, Wolfsburg
If you plan to head out to Wolfsburg, this is worth seeing in its own right, with or without a visit to Autostadt. The sheer size and design of this building makes it one of the more exciting things to see, even if you don't step inside. Adjacent to the

🔺 *'Liquid Mirror' exhibition at the Phaeno Science Centre*

railway station, the Centre was designed by award-winning London-based architect Zaha Hadid at the beginning of the millennium. On offer are exhibits and presentations about the sciences, especially physics, biology and chemistry plus more futuristic concepts. There is a good restaurant in the grounds of this ode to all things scientific. ❷ Willy-Brandt-Pl. 1 ❶ 0180 016 06 00 ❺ www.phaeno.de ❹ 09.00–17.00 Tues–Fri, 10.00–18.00 Sat & Sun ❾ DB or ICE Train: Wolfsburg. Admission charge

Mines of Rammelsberg & Goslar

Since 1992, these have been a joint UNESCO World Heritage Site.

Mines of Rammelsberg Once the largest interconnected deposits of metal ore in the world, these former mines now house a museum dedicated to the history of local ore extraction. The mines were open for over 1,000 years, with over 27 million tonnes of ore extracted. They closed in 1988, when the ore was exhausted. ❷ Bergtal 19 ❶ 05321 75 00 ❺ www.rammelsberg.de ❹ 09.00–18.00 ❾ DB Train: Rammelsberg

Historic town of Goslar The town of Goslar has important historical connections because of its role in the Hanseatic League. From the 10th to the 12th centuries, it was one of the seats of the Holy Roman Empire of the German Nation. Suffering little damage during World War II, over 1,500 half-timbered houses are to be found in the historic medieval centre, some up to 400 years old. **Goslar Tourism Office** ❷ Markt 7, Goslar ❶ 05321 780 60 ❺ www.goslar.de ❾ DB Train: Goslar

Rausch Schokoland (Chocolate Land), Peine

Rausch is one of the best chocolate brands in Germany: produced in Lower Saxony for 24 years, although established in 1890, this is good stuff. Chocolate Land is a chocoholic's dream. Museum, playland and factory tours are all available. Learn about the history of not only the Rausch family and the company, but also about the medicinal use of the cacao tree and its role in Aztec culture. Plan nearly a whole day for an excursion, or include it as a part of a trip out to Peine. ⓐ Wilhelm-Rausch-Str. 4, Peine ⓣ 05171 990 120 ⓦ www.rausch-schokolade.de/schokoland ⓛ 10.00–18.00 Mon–Fri, 10.00–16.00 Sat, 12.00–17.00 Sun ⓝ DB Train: Peine

Telemax Radio Tower

This impressive telecommunications tower is operated by Deutsche Telekom. Including the 10 m (33 ft) base, this 282 m (925 ft) structure, built from 1988 to 1992, is lit up when large trade fairs are in town. Designer Hans U. Boeckler received the cement-steel prize *Die Kunst des Bewehrens* for it. Can be seen from all over the city, but especially from the A2 direction, Lehrte or the Messe. ⓐ Hannover Buchholz-Kleefeld

EAST OF HANOVER
European Cheese Centre

Do you like cheese? The people at the European Cheese Centre certainly do and boast of being the only cheese experience centre in Europe. Come along one evening and learn all there is to know about *Käse* (cheese) and taste your way around the Continent. ⓐ Hägenstr. 13 ⓣ 586 66 26 ⓦ www.cheese-center.de

◆ *Half-timbered houses on Goslar's Marktplatz*

🕐 From 18.30 Wed & 18.00 or 19.00 Thur, and sometimes on Tues & Sat Ⓝ U-Bahn: Bahnhof Anderten/Misburg

Excalibur Hannover

Meat eaters and those in love with the Middle Ages will appreciate this unique restaurant in one of the more exclusive parts of the city. Your meals will be delivered to your table by maidens and knights. Although there is not much on offer for vegetarians, this is a fun night out for the whole family. ⓐ Bemeroder Rathauspl. 1 ☏ 525 655 ⓦ www.excalibur-hannover.de 🕐 18.30–00.00 Wed–Sat Ⓝ U-Bahn: Bemeroder/Mitte

Tiergarten

Not your normal *Tiergarten* (zoo). This free, open-air zoo gives local wild animals the chance to roam in less confined spaces. There is a playground near the U-Bahn entrance, a beer garden close by, as well as a restaurant in a nearby hotel. The festival held here in autumn is a real treat for children. Also a good place for a stroll if you are staying locally, or need something less jam-packed than the Maschsee (see page 34). If you do make it out here, take a look around at the beautiful homes, some former farming estates, in this exclusive and wealthy neighbourhood. ⓐ Tiergartenstr. 149 🕐 07.00–dusk Feb–mid-Nov; 11.00–dusk Mon–Thur, 07.00–dusk Fri–Sun, mid-Nov–Jan Ⓝ U-Bahn: Tiergarten

▶ *Altes Rathaus and St Mary's Church, Celle*

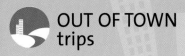

Celle

Northeast of Hanover, Celle is a city over 700 years old, and saturated with quaint charm. Historic, medieval and antique – this city maintained much of its old-school splendour after World War II. What Hanover lacks in historic elegance, Celle offers in abundance. No trip to Hanover is complete without a trip up north, so be sure to make your way to Celle if you have the time.

GETTING THERE

Celle is 40 km (25 miles) northeast of Hanover, and is well served by DB trains, which leave several times an hour. Travelling to Celle by S-Bahn or regional train takes 25–45 minutes each way, depending upon the time of day and the train's final destination. Tickets cost around €10 each way. Travel by IC train takes less than 20 minutes each way and costs a few euros more.

However, if you plan to stay only for the day, your best bet with train travel to Celle is the Niedersachsen Ticket. This ticket costs about €20 for single travellers, but is only €27 for a group of up to five adults, plus two children (that's up to seven travellers in total). This ticket allows you or your group to travel to any destination within Niedersachsen, including Hamburg and Bremen, from 09.00 on the day of departure to 03.00 the next day, Monday to Saturday. On Sundays and holidays, travel time is 00.00 on the day of departure until 03.00 the next day. Train travel is restricted to regional trains (IRE, RE, RB and S-Bahn). The ticket also includes use of public transport in the destination city during the time of validity. See Ⓦ www.bahn.de for more information.

SIGHTS & ATTRACTIONS

Many of the sights and attractions in Celle are close to each other. Grab a city map and explore all this beautiful city has to offer. Admission is free, unless otherwise stated.

Altstadt Celle

Be sure to bring extra film or an extra memory card for your camera when you venture through the old town in Celle. Over 500 half-timbered houses nestle in the old town. Best strolls are along Neuestrasse and Zöllnerstrasse. And check out the Rathaus.

BERGEN-BELSEN MEMORIAL

Located about 20 km (12 miles) northwest of Celle, in the Lüneburg Heath. This former prisoner-of-war and concentration camp was in full operation from 1940 to 1945. By its close on 15 April 1945, over 70,000 people had been killed. In memory of those killed and tortured here, there are marked graves as well as monuments and exhibits. Learn more about the victims and the camp itself in the documentation centre. It is best accessed by car, but public transport is also available; there are numerous buses to Bergen from Celle railway station.
ⓐ Gedenkstätte Bergen-Belsen, D-29303 Lohheide
ⓣ 05051 475 90 ⓦ www.bergen-belsen.de ⓒ 10.00–18.00 Apr–Sept; 10.00–17.00 Oct–Mar

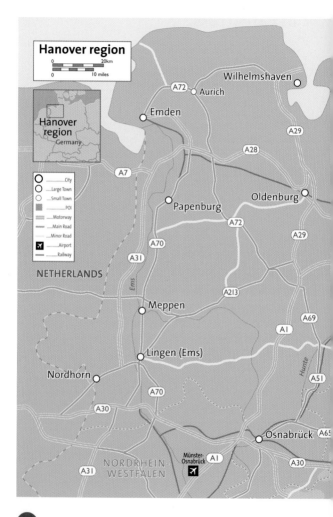

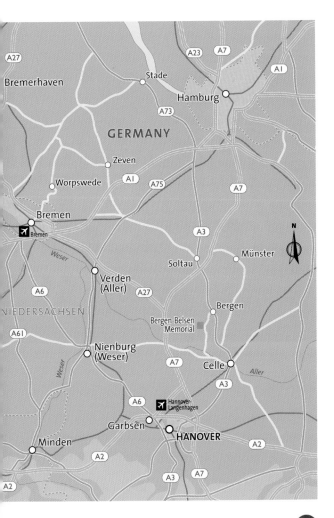

◔ *The castle – the pride of Celle*

Celle Castle

One of the most outstanding castles in Germany. The Dukes
of Braunschweig-Lüneburg made Celle their home in 1378;
however, the original building dates back to the 13th century
and was completed in Renassiance style in the early 1530s, by
Duke Ernst der Bekenner. The castle was given its current look
in the 18th century by avid art lover Georg Wilhelm. The eastern

façade of the castle has octagonal towers and gables. Mesmerising when illuminated at night. ⓐ Schlosspl., Celle ⓣ 05141 123 73 ⓛ 10.00–16.00 Apr–Oct. Groups of over 15 must make a reservation. Admission charge

Celle Synagogue
This is the oldest surviving half-timbered synagogue in northern Germany. Look out for changing exhibits on Jewish life, especially

in Germany, Lower Saxony and Celle. ⓐ Im Kreise 23–24
ⓣ 05141 12 12 ⓛ 12.00–17.00 Tues–Thur, 09.00–14.00 Fri,
11.00–14.00 Sun, closed on Jewish high holidays.
Call ahead for a 60-minute guided tour

Celler Badeland

Just as the name implies, this venture is filled with places to
swim, bathe and enjoy being wet. Great for singles, couples or
the entire family, Celler Badeland is about the size of six football
pitches. Activities range from saunas (no swimming costumes
allowed), a giant chute, indoor and outdoor swimming pools
plus whirlpools and numerous sports facilities. ⓐ 77er Str., Celle
ⓣ 05141 951 95 30 ⓦ www.celler-badeland.de ⓛ Vary: call ahead
for more info ⓝ Bus: 5. Admission charge

🔺 *A peaceful spot in the French Garden*

French Garden

Specially made for Celle's Duke Georg Wilhelm, this garden has gone through several stages of greatness and tragedy. Today's garden is a nice place for a walk or to sit and picnic for lunch. Children's playground on site. ⓐ Main entrance is on Magnusstr. ⓛ Sunrise–sunset

Heilpflanzengarten (Medicinal Plant Garden), Celle

One of the largest of its kind in Europe, this is great for horticulture fans and those interested in the plants used in common medicines. Café KräuThae on site uses plants grown in nearby gardens. There's also a gift shop. ⓐ Wittinger Str. 76 ⓣ 05141 208 173 ⓦ www.heilpflanzen-garten.de ⓛ 10.00–18.00 Mar–Nov

Stadtkirche (St Mary's Church)

Hear that music coming from the church tower? It's not the latest pop music super hit, it's the Celle town trumpeter. After climbing the 74.5 m (244 ft) tower twice a day, the trumpeter blasts the city with the same tune as others have for centuries. You can make the same trek up the 235 stairs for fantastic views of Celle. The church has changed architectural styles twice in its history – it was first a Gothic church, now it's a baroque one. Visit the crypt for a glimpse of the remains of royalty. ⓐ An der Stadtkirche 8 ⓦ www.stadtkirche-celle.de ⓛ 10.00–18.00. Admission charge

Tourist Information Office

Provides a full range of information on things to see and do in town and in the Celle region, plus free maps and local transport info. Accommodation booking services are also on offer.

ⓐ Marktpl. 14–16 ☎ 05141 12 12 🕐 09.00–18.00 Mon–Fri, 10.00–16.00 Sat, 11.00–14.00 Sun, 15 May–15 Oct; 09.00–17.00 Mon–Fri, 10.00–13.00 Sat, 16 Oct–14 May ⓦ www.region-celle.de

CULTURE

Bomann-Museum

This is the third-largest museum in Lower Saxony, with the history of Lower Saxony and Celle its main attraction. ⓐ Schlosspl. 7 ☎ 05141 123 72 ⓦ www.bomann-museum.de 🕐 10.00–17.00 Tues–Sun

Eberhard Schlotter Foundation

Housed in the Bomann-Museum, this foundation is responsible for maintaining the legacy of painter and graphic artist Eberhard Schlotter. An expansive collection of his works are on permanent display. Same contact details as for Bomann-Museum above.

Kunstmuseum Celle/Erstes 24-Stunden-Kunstmuseum der Welt

Home to illuminated art, contemporary paintings and sculptures. This is the world's first 24-hour art museum: check out the light installations on the front of the museum at night. Same contact details as for Bomann-Museum above. ⓦ www.kunst.celle.de

RETAIL THERAPY

Farmers' Market Explore the vibrant farmers' market in the celebrated city centre on Wednesdays and Saturdays. Follow the crowds to Marktplatz.

Explore the history of Lower Saxony at the Bomann-Museum

Zöllnerstrasse Celle's high street. Most of the city's shopping is hidden within the half-timbered buildings in the centre.

AFTER DARK

RESTAURANTS

Historischer Ratskeller ££ One of the oldest (and nicest) pubs in Lower Saxony, built in 1378. Located in the basement of the Rathaus, this is the perfect place to relax after a day of sightseeing. Most of the menu is German, with simple but hearty dishes of beef and several varieties of pork – pork roast, pork *Schnitzel* and *Wurst*. There is an above average list of beers, wines and non-alcoholic drinks on the menu. ⓐ Markt 14 ⓣ 05141 290 99 ⓦ www.ratskeller-celle.de ⓛ 11.30–14.30, 17.30–00.00 Mon–Sat, 11.30–14.30 Sun

Weinkeller Postmeister von Hinüber ££ Located in the old town, this restaurant reflects the locals' affinity for wine, with an international selection. The seasonal menu also includes a special menu card every week. Past main dishes have included crème of kohlrabi soup with liver and truffle oil. Enjoy the yummy freshly baked bread or try the peach mascarpone cake with dark chocolate sauce for dessert. Call ahead and make a reservation. ⓐ Zöllnerstr. 25 ⓣ 05141 284 44 ⓦ www.weinkeller-celle.de ⓛ 18.00–00.00 Tues–Fri, 12.00–14.00, 18.00–00.00 Sat

Endtenfang £££ This restaurant, located inside the hotel Fürstenhof Celle, is one of the poshest places to dine in Celle – come here for a splurge. The menu features game and pork; and, as the name suggests, duck is one of the house specialities. Root

CELLE WINE MARKET
One of the events in Celle's annual calendar, when the wine producers from the area and region bring in their finest samples. Usually held in spring or early summer.
☎ 05141 12 12 ⓦ www.region-celle.com

vegetables and apples make delectable side dishes. The wine list is excellent, as are the desserts. Well worth a visit. ⓐ Hanoversche Str. 55/56 ☎ 05141 201 177 ⓦ www.fuerstenhof-celle.com
🕑 12.00–14.00, 18.00–22.00 Mon–Sat

ACCOMMODATION

Deutsches Jugendherbergswerk £ Celle's one hostel is run by the German arm of Hostelling International.
ⓐ Weghausstr. 2 ☎ 05141 532 308 ⓦ www.jugendherberge.de

Tryp Celle ££ There are 126 rooms at this 3-star hotel located outside the old town. There is a 24-hour bar on site and a Spanish-themed restaurant. ⓐ Fuhrberger Str. 6, Celle ☎ 05141 97 20

Fürstenhof Celle £££ This is the finest place to sleep in Celle. Dating back to the 18th century, this inn is located inside one of Celle's many half-timbered houses. Sixty-three rooms and 123 beds are here for your enjoyment and a restful night's sleep. ⓐ Hannoversche Str. 55/56 ☎ 05141 20 10 ⓦ www.fuerstenhof-celle.com

Bremen

Bremen is one of Germany's three city-states, with a population of over 600,000. It combines city and provincial life, trade and influence as a major port city and its role in the Hanseatic League with old town architecture and art museums, making for a worthwhile and interesting visit.

GETTING THERE

Bremen is 129 km (80 miles) northwest of Hanover, and is well served by public transport, with DB trains leaving several times an hour. Travel to Bremen by S-Bahn or regional train takes 1½ hours each way, depending on the time of day and the train's final destination. Tickets cost less than €20 each way. Travel by IC or ICE train takes less than an hour each way and costs about €5–10 more.

However, your best bet with train travel to Bremen, if you plan to stay only for the day, is the Niedersachsen Ticket (see page 104 and ⓦ www.bahn.de for more information).

SIGHTS & ATTRACTIONS

Becks Brewery and tours

Bremen is the home town of one of Germany's and the world's most popular beers – Becks. Although the factory was sold to InBev in 2002, it remains one of the brands strongly associated with northern Germany. Factory tours include samples along with info on the history of the brewery. ⓐ Brauerei Beck GmbH & Co, Am Deich 18/19 ⓣ 0421 509 40 ⓦ www.becks.de

BÖTTCHERSTRASSE – STREET ART

Converted into a magnificent place for a stroll by coffee merchant Ludwig Roselius in 1926–30, this street was preserved by the National Socialists as an example of degenerate art. Here you will also find the Paula Becker-Modersohn exhibition and Roselius Museum. The front entrance features a bas-relief of the Archangel Michael fighting a dragon.

🕐 Tour times: 12.30, 14.00, 15.30, 17.00 Thur–Sat, Jan–Mar; 11.00, 12.30, 14.00, 15.30, 17.00 Thur & Fri, 09.30, 11.00, 12.30, 14.00, 15.30, 17.00 Sat, Apr–Dec. Admission charge

Bremen Tourist Information Office

Located away from Marktplatz, this should be your first stop for maps, river cruise schedules and public transport info. An accommodation booking service is also available. ⓐ At the main train station ☎ 01805 101 030 ⓦ www.bremen-tourism.de/english/frame 🕐 09.00–19.00 Mon–Fri, 09.30–18.00 Sat & Sun

Die Bremer Stadtmusikanten (The Town Musicians)

On the west side of the town hall, this life-like statue is dedicated to the larger than life Brothers Grimm story. Tired of being taken for granted, four animals – a dog, cat, donkey and rooster – head to Bremen, a town known for its independence. The animals stand on each other's backs and were created by Gerhard Marcks in 1953 (see page 123).

Marktplatz

The heart of Bremen's Altstadt (old town). Come here to see the cathedral, gabled houses and Rathaus (town hall). In front of the Rathaus note the over-600-year-old, 10 m (32 ft) statue of Roland, a symbol of independence. He faces the cathedral, warning the bishop to watch his step.

Ports of Bremen and Bremerhaven

The ports in Bremen and Bremerhaven see some of the busiest shipping action in Europe. Take a walk along the boardwalk or check out Neustädter Hafen in Bremen and the container terminal in Bremerhaven, which is the biggest vehicle trans-shipment facility in Europe. Also a good bet is the Columbus Quay, once a point of departure for European emigrants.

Rhododendron-Park und Botanischer Garten

A horticultural explosion of rhododendrons with a total of over 450 species, 350 subspecies and 350 azalea varieties. Also check out the 250 species of related evergreen plants, and Bürgerpark, an English-style garden dating back to 1865. Near the city centre.
ⓐ Marcusallee 60 ⓣ 0421 361 30 25 ⓦ www.rhodo.org/park.php
ⓛ 07.30–sunset; May–Sept is the best time to go

St Petri Dom (St Peter's Cathedral)

The oldest church in Bremen. Gothic in style, its two towers are 98 m (320 ft) high. The cathedral was built between the 11th and 13th centuries. Original parts of the church remained undamaged during World War II and are still in place today. Check out the mummified remains of local bigwigs, all encased in glass: a bit

⏺ *Degenerate art on Böttcherstrasse*

creepy, but intriguing as well. The museum also on the premises provides more information on the history of the church and Catholicism in the area.

The so-called Spitting Stone may not sound like a hygienic place to visit, but it is a local tradition nonetheless. Located on the west side of St Peter's Cathedral, this stone is the place

◗ *Marktplatz – with its stone statue of Roland*

where the mass-murderer Gesche Gottfried died. She was the last person to be publicly executed in Bremen and locals hock up their best and aim for the stone to show their disgust at her actions.

As you walk into the church, you may see a young man sweeping the church steps. Local tradition requires all unmarried men on their 30th birthday to sweep the church steps until they

receive a kiss from a young female passer-by. ⓐ Sandstr. 10–12
ⓘ 0421 365 040 ⓦ www.stpetridom.de ⓛ 10.00–17.00 Mon–Fri,
10.00–14.00 Sat, 14.00–17.00 Sun

'Schaffer' Banquet

This, the oldest men-only banquet in the world, is held every
February for the men in Bremen to attend in order to 'come out
as men'. At least that was the case when the tradition began
back in 1545. Now it's held more for the traditional and cultural
aspects: like a big pow-wow for the men in the city plus their
sons. For male non-citizens of Bremen this is a once-in-a-
lifetime experience. Formal attire is essential when you join
your 'brothers' at the Neptune table, to celebrate the end
of winter, beginning of spring and new business prospects.
Traditional menu consists of Bremen chicken soup, malty
'sailor's beer', salt cod and kale with *Pinkel*. Contact the tourist
information office for more information on exact dates and
locations. ⓦ www.schaffermahlzeit.de

Schnoorviertel

What a difference a few hundred years make! The houses in this
area of the old town, dating to the 15th and 18th centuries, were
formerly occupied by working-class residents of Bremen. Left
almost undamaged by World War II, the area is now home to
some of the city's most exclusive restaurants, shops and cafés.

Schütting

Located on the southwestern side of the Marktplatz, this former
mansion used by the Merchants' Guild was built in Flemish-

The fabled Town Musicians, immortalised in bronze

inspired Renaissance architectural style in 1537–8. It is currently the city's chamber of commerce. Am Markt 13 0421 363 70

Worpswede

This village northeast of Bremen is a well-known former artists' colony celebrated for its famous painters, poets and architects – and their subsequent influence on Expressionism. The village boomed as a hotbed of creativity from the late 19th century until the end of World War II. Paula Becker-Modersohn, Fritz Mackensen, Otto Modersohn and Hans am Ende are famous past residents. Check out some of the local architecture such as the Worpswede Käseglocke. To get to Worpswede, take Bus 670 from the Bremen Hauptbahnhof; the journey takes about an hour.

CULTURE

Kunsthalle

Art gallery on the outskirts of the old town. Much of its artistic heritage was lost to Russia but what remains is nonetheless of significance. Works by Rembrandt, Monet, Denis and Beckmann. Also, many works by Paula Becker-Modersohn. Am Wall 207 0421 329 080 www.kunsthalle-bremen.de 10.00–21.00 Tues, 10.00–17.00 Wed–Sun

Überseemuseum

Germany was one of the countries that built its wealth in former times through colonisation and imperialism in Africa, present-day Namibia being one of its conquests. Dedicated to the culture of non-European nations, this museum displays artefacts from former German colonies, but also forces its visitors to take a more considered look at the effects of colonialism and imperialism. ⓐ Bahnhofpl. 13 ⓣ 0421 160 381 90 ⓦ www.uebersee-museum.de ⓛ 09.00–18.00 Mon–Fri, 10.00–18.00 Sat & Sun. Admission charge

RETAIL THERAPY

Space Shop Located in the airport near the visitors' platform. The unique offerings are out of this world. Come here to find items relating to space exploration and space travel. Items include meteorites and even an astronaut's suit. ⓐ Bremen International Airport ⓣ 0421 559 57 88 ⓛ 10.00–18.00 ⓝ U-Bahn: Bremen Flughafen

TAKE A BREAK

Café Tölke The place to try the famous Viennese *Sachertorte* or enjoy a relaxing cup of coffee. Also good for lunch. ⓐ Am Landerrnamt 1 ⓣ 0421 324 330 ⓛ 10.00–00.00

AFTER DARK

When it is in season, be sure to catch the local speciality *Kohl und Pinkel*. This dish comprises green, curly kale and hearty helpings of various meats, one of which is usually *Pinkel* sausage (pig's intestine filled with oatmeal).

RESTAURANTS

Topaz £–££ Bistro-style cuisine with a classy (and not too expensive) feel, a large list of wines (some rather expensive ones, too) and a nest in the Kontorhaus, right in the heart of the city. ⓐ Langenstr. 2–4 ⓣ 0421 776 25 ⓦ www.topaz-bremen.de. ⓛ 12.00–21.30 Mon–Fri, 12.00–15.00 Sat

Bremer Ratskeller ££ Traditional Bremen cuisine. ⓐ Am Markt ⓣ 0421 321 676 ⓛ 11.00–00.00 Mon–Sat

ACCOMMODATION

Mercure Hotel Hanseatic Bremen £ Three-star chain hotel with free parking. Not far from the centre. ⓐ Neuenlander Str. 55 ⓣ 0421 522 680 ⓦ www.mercure-hotel-hanseatic-bremen.de

Hilton Bremen ££ Air-conditioning in all 235 rooms. On the famous Böttcherstrasse. ⓐ Böttcherstr. 2 ⓣ 0421 369 60 ⓦ www.hilton.de/bremen

Park Hotel Bremen £££ One of the most luxurious hotels in Germany. Its spa facilities are well known. ⓐ Im Bürgerpark ⓣ 0421 340 80 ⓦ www.park-hotel-bremen.de

ⓞ *The Hauptbahnhof – all trains arrive here*

PRACTICAL information

Directory

GETTING THERE
By air

Hanover is served by one airport, Hannover-Langenhagen Airport (HAJ) (☎ 977 12 23 or 12 24 ⓦ www.hannover-airport.de) which is located 11 km (7 miles) northwest of the city centre in Langenhagen.

Air Berlin ☎ 01805 737 800 ⓦ www.airberlin.com
Lufthansa ☎ 01805 838 426 ⓦ www.lufthansa.com
British Airways ☎ 01805 266 522 ⓦ www.britishairways.com
Air France ☎ 01805 830 830 ⓦ www.airfrance.com
TUIfly ☎ 01805 757 510 ⓦ www.tuifly.com

Many people are aware that air travel emits CO_2, which contributes to climate change. You may be interested in the possibility of lessening the environmental impact of your flight through the charity **Climate Care** (ⓦ www.climatecare.org), which offsets your CO_2 by funding environmental projects around the world.

There is only one train line from the airport, S5, which takes you to the Hauptbahnhof in the centre of town. Travel time from the airport to the railway station is 12 minutes and costs approx €2.50 per person for each trip.

The 470 bus from the airport travels to the Langenhagen-Mitte S-Bahn station but travel time is much longer and the cost is the same.

When you reach the city, stick to either the blue or red public transport maps, depending upon which type of ticket you buy.

Make sure you validate your ticket on the U-Bahn platform or on the train. You could be fined otherwise.

Currency exchange is available at Sparkasse Bank and Travelex offices in Terminal A.

By rail

Trains to Hanover leave from London St Pancras International Station. Standard journey time is about nine hours and part of the journey is on the Eurostar. Tickets can be purchased at London St Pancras International Station.

Trains arrive at Hannover Hauptbahnhof (main railway station), but during international trade fairs, some trains from major cities also stop at the Hannover Messe/Laatzen station and at the Messegelände (fair grounds), in the southwest of the city.

The German train system is efficient, and rail staff will validate your tickets on the train themselves.

DB offers several ticket options for those travelling in Germany. If your stay in Hanover is part of a larger German excursion, look into one of the many rail passes or the DB Bahn Cards. The DB Bahn Cards are saver cards that allow passengers to save up to 50 per cent on train tickets or pay one lump sum for train travel for the entire year.

By road

The minimum age for driving in Germany is 18. Foreign drivers require a valid licence and proof of insurance. A country identification sticker must be displayed on the vehicle.

Germany has a brilliant network of Autobahnen (motorways, prefixed 'A') and Bundesstrassen (major roads, prefixed 'B').

Traffic drives on the right with speed limits of 130 kph (80 mph) or 100 kph (62 mph) outside built-up areas; 50 kph (31 mph) is the limit in built-up areas; there are no speed limits on Autobahnen. Hanover is accessed by the A2 and B3.

Seatbelts must be worn at all times and children under 12 years can only travel in the front seat with a child restraint.

German laws are strict by many accounts when it comes to driving under the influence of alcohol. The legal maximum alcohol to blood ratio for driving is 0.05%.

ENTRY FORMALITIES

Germany is a member of the EU. UK and other citizens of EU member countries require only a valid identity card or passport for entry. EU citizens may stay in Germany without a visa for an unspecified amount of time.

EU citizens are permitted to bring any goods back home from Germany at their discretion as long as they are for personal use, excluding tobacco and alcohol. Tobacco limits are 200 cigarettes and alcohol is limited to one litre over 22 per cent by volume.

TRAVEL INSURANCE

Those requiring travel insurance should head to one of the TUI Reise Centers. There is one at the airport and several in town. The closest one to the centre is located at ⓐ Georgstr. 16 ⓣ 301 90 ⓦ www.tui-reisecenter24.de

Contact the national travel centre on ⓣ 01805 884 266 for more information.

South Africans need a visa to enter Germany. Citizens of the USA, Canada, Republic of Ireland and New Zealand do not require visas for stays up to 90 days. Citizens from these countries are allowed to bring goods back home from Germany at their discretion as long as they are for personal use, excluding tobacco and alcohol. Tobacco limits are 200 cigarettes and alcohol is limited one litre over 22 per cent by volume.

MONEY

The euro (€) is the official currency in Germany. Most currency exchange bureaux are located at the airport, the main railway station and at the banks on Bahnhofstrasse. Some of the other banks in the centre offer currency exchange and international wire transfers, but call ahead for service times. Some of the larger hotels also offer currency exchange services.

Credit cards are not widely accepted as a means of payment. Although the EC Karte, a European debit bank card, is more widely accepted, it is always best to ask before shopping to see if the store of your choice accepts it as a method of payment. Cash is accepted and preferred by most merchants.

HEALTH, SAFETY & CRIME

Hanover is a relatively safe city, except for some seedy areas around the railway station and near Steintor after the sun goes down. As always, it is good practice to be aware of your surroundings at all times of the day and stick to main roads if you are unfamiliar with the area.

Pickpockets and petty thieves are not as common in the more touristy areas as one might expect, but none the less

beware. Petty theft rates rise when trade fairs are in town –
especially CeBIT – or when sporting events are on such as
Hannover 96 matches.

If you are a victim of a crime, report this at the main police
station in the Hauptbahnhof. The entrance is level with the
Hauptbahnhof's main entrance, but to the far left, just before
the tunnel under the railway tracks. Look for the police vans and
cars outside.

Although not common practice among locals, drinking the
water in Hanover is safe to do, but bottled water is obviously
available everywhere.

Food standards are high and many items on the German
menu are required to follow certain strict purity standards.
German laws require preservatives and colourings to not only
be noted on menus and food labels but also be specified by
their exact scientific ID number.

All travellers are advised to bring medication for tummy
upsets, should they have sensitive stomachs.

OPENING HOURS

One thing can be said for the opening hours in Hanover, the
early bird definitely gets the worm. Attractions, offices, shops
and markets are more likely to be open earlier than later and
most do not stay open late for customers. Do not under any
circumstances plan to arrive just before closing. Not only will
you attract glares from the shopkeepers, you may not even be
let into the shop.

Larger stores and supermarkets are open Monday to Friday
09.00–20.00 and on Saturday 09.00–16.00. Smaller shops stay

open until 18.30 during the week and until 14.00 on Saturday.

Most museums are closed on Mondays and have one day a week, usually Fridays, where admission is free or reduced for the whole or part of the day. Hanover is a university town and many attractions and cultural venues offer concessions for students. It is always best to call ahead for more information.

Offices are usually open Monday to Friday 08.00–17.00, with an hour for lunch around 13.00. If calling an office, be sure to state your last name first. It is more common in Germany to be called by your last name by strangers or acquaintances so when calling anywhere by phone, it is expected that you announce yourself first.

Banks normally open from 08.00–17.00 Monday to Friday, with those outside the centre closing for an hour for lunch around 13.00. Some banks have weekend hours, usually from 08.00–13.00.

TOILETS

If you need a toilet, head to one of the department stores such as Kaufhof, Karstadt or to Kaufland. They are normally staffed and it is considered polite to tip the attendant 10–30 cents for use of the facilities.

CHILDREN

Hanover can be a mecca for travelling families and is a family-friendly city. Many hotels offer cots and play areas. Many attractions offer tickets and events especially for kids. Child seats and child portions are common in restaurants. Children up to six usually travel for free with the cost of a paying adult ticket on DB trains and on ÜSTRA services.

● *Children will enjoy seeing the elephants at Hanover Zoo*

However, it is considered quite rude to bring children into smarter restaurants for dinner in the evenings. If you have children, plan ahead and ring your destination eatery to ask if children are permitted in the evenings.

Convenience items such as baby food and nappies can be bought in every drug store such as Rossmann and DM, and in grocery stores.

To keep children occupied, the best options in town are Hanover Zoo (see page 77), the Tiergarten (see page 102) and the events at the Grosser Garten. Look for the Little Festival there in summer (see page 12).

COMMUNICATIONS

Internet

Internet cafés are common and can be found all over town. Stick to the ones in student or immigrant-dominated areas for the lowest prices. **Tele Baba** (ⓐ Limmerstr. 69 ⓣ 169 92 60) has the lowest prices in town at approx €1/hour.

Phones

Pay phones accept coins and cards, and the cleanest ones are in post offices. Unless otherwise specified, 0511 is the prefix for all Hanover numbers and does not need to be dialled if you are calling from within the city limits. Phone numbers vary in length, so don't worry if you see anything from three to nine digits.

Most mobiles from European countries will work in Germany, but most from the USA and Canada will not. Check with your service provider first if you are from the USA or Canada and want to use your mobile phone.

TELEPHONING GERMANY

The city area code for Hanover is 0511. If calling Hanover from abroad, dial the country code 49 for Germany, drop the first zero, press 5-1-1 and then the rest of the number.

TELEPHONING ABROAD

Dial 00, the country code, the area code and the local number. Dialling codes: Australia 61; Canada 1; Ireland 353; New Zealand 64; South Africa 27; UK 44; USA 1.

Post

Postal services in Germany are efficient and widespread. Deutsche Post offices are everywhere: look out for the yellow signs noting their locations. Most post office branches also act as DHL logistic centres and Postbank branches.

Stamps can be bought from tobacconists and from machines at post offices. Single stamps for international postage cannot be bought from machines, so you will have to queue up.

ELECTRICITY

Voltage in Germany is 220 volts for electrical appliances. Electrical appliances from the UK and the rest of Europe will need a plug adapter for two round pins.

Electrical appliances from the USA and Canada will need a voltage converter to change the voltage from 110 volts to 220 volts, as well as a plug adapter.

If you find yourself in Hanover without the required gear, head to **Saturn** (ⓐ Ernst-August-Pl. 3 ⓣ 450 20 ⓛ 10.00–20.00 Ⓝ U-Bahn: Hauptbahnhof) or **Conrad Electronic** (ⓐ Goseriede 3 ⓣ 177 49 ⓛ 10.00–20.00 ⓦ www.conrad.de Ⓝ U-Bahn: Steintor).

TRAVELLERS WITH DISABILITIES

Generally speaking Hanover is decently equipped for travellers with disabilities. Most pavements have dropped kerbs, the Hauptbahnhof has material in Braille and all underground ÜSTRA stations have lifts. Visit ⓦ www.niedersachsen-tourism.de/en/specials for more information on special tourism options for those with disabilities.

TOURIST INFORMATION

Hanover Tourist Information Office Souvenirs, especially books about the city and local magazines, plus free events listings – although all are in German. Buy the 'Red Thread' booklet here for approx €2 and other materials in English. Also books rooms and sells tickets for events. ⓐ Ernst-August-Pl. 8 ⓣ 123 451 11 ⓦ www.hannover.de ⓝ U-Bahn: Hauptbahnhof ⓛ 09.00–18.00 Mon–Fri, 09.00–14.00 Sat; also 09.00–14.00 Sun, Apr–Oct

BACKGROUND READING

German Women's Movement: Class and Gender in Hanover, 1880–1933 by Nancy R. Reagin. The effect of the Women's Movement in Hanover.

Hanoverian London by George Rude. Explores life in 18th-century England under Hanoverian rule.

Hanoverians: The History of a Dynasty by Jeremy Black. More on Hanover's link to the British throne.

So Schön ist Hannover by Jörg A. Fischer and Wolfgang Steinweg. Photo book with text in three languages (German, English and French) about the history and highlights of Hanover.

Emergencies

The following are emergency free-call numbers:
Fire brigade ❶ 112 **Police** ❶ 110 **Emergency doctors** Central
❶ 380 380, Children's ❶ 380 300 **Emergency dentists** ❶ 311 031

MEDICAL SERVICES

If you become ill while in Hanover, contact the staff of your hotel.
Many local medical services provide up-to-date information to
hotels etc., due to the large number of international visitors
Hanover hosts year round. Lists of English-speaking medical
providers can also be found by contacting your local consulate
or at one of the chemists where staff speak English. For hospitals,
try the following – they have a special English-speaking unit:
Hospital-Henriettenstiftung ⓐ Marienstr. 72–90 ❶ 28 90
Vinzenzkrankenhaus Hannover ⓐ Lange-Feld-Str. 31 ❶ 95 00

For an English-speaking doctor, try **Dr K-H Schuckert**
(ⓐ Ellernstr. 23 ❶ 810 831).

The chemist inside the railway station is open on Sundays
but with limited hours. If you need a prescription filled, contact
the tourist information office or the emergency doctor: by law,
at least one chemist in Hanover is required to open its doors
on Sundays.

Both of the large chemists near the railway station have
English-speaking staff:
Löwen Apotheke ⓐ Bahnhofstr. 2 ❶ 0800 48 48 48 2 (free call)
Ⓦ www.loewen-apotheke-hannover.de
Ernst August Apotheke ⓐ Bahnhofstr. 8 ❶ 363 432
Ⓦ www.ernst-august.de

POLICE

If you are the victim of petty crime, including having your
passport stolen, report the crime immediately to the police.

Polizeistation Raschplatz ⓐ Raschpl. 11-CG ☎ 109 60 15

EMBASSIES & CONSULATES

Australian Embassy ⓐ Wallstr. 76–79, Berlin ☎ (030) 880 08 80
ⓦ www.germany.embassy.gov.au

Canadian Embassy ⓐ Friedrichstr. 95, Berlin ☎ (030) 20 31 20
ⓦ www.international.gc.ca/canada-europa/germany

New Zealand Embassy ⓐ Friedrichstr. 60, Berlin ☎ (030) 20 62 10
ⓦ www.nzembassy.com

UK Consulate ⓐ Karl Wiechert Allee 50 ☎ 388 38 08 ⓦ www.fco.gov.uk

United States Embassy ⓐ Neustädtische Kirchstr. 4–5, Berlin
☎ (030) 238 51 74 ⓦ germany.usembassy.gov

EMERGENCY PHRASES

Help!	**Fire!**	**Stop!**
Hilfe!	Feuer!	Halt!
Heelfe!	*Foyer!*	*Halt!*

Call an ambulance/a doctor/the police/the fire service, please!
Rufen Sie bitte einen Krankenwagen/einen Arzt/
die Polizei/die Feuerwehr!
Roofen zee bitter inen krankenvaagen/inen artst/
dee politsye/dee foyervair!

SPOTTED YOUR NEXT CITY BREAK?

...then these lightweight CitySpots pocket guides will have you in the know in no time, wherever you're heading.

Covering over 90 cities worldwide, they're packed with detail on the most important urban attractions from shopping and sights to non-stop nightlife; knocking spots off chunkier, clunkier versions.

Aarhus	Gdansk	Oslo
Amsterdam	Geneva	Palermo
Antwerp	Genoa	Palma
Athens	Glasgow	Paris
Bangkok	Gothenburg	Pisa
Barcelona	Granada	Prague
Belfast	Hamburg	Porto
Belgrade	Hanover	Reykjavik
Berlin	Helsinki	Riga
Biarritz	Hong Kong	Rome
Bilbao	Istanbul	Rotterdam
Bologna	Kiev	Salzburg
Bordeaux	Krakow	Sarajevo
Bratislava	Kuala Lumpur	Seville
Bruges	Leipzig	Singapore
Brussels	Lille	Sofia
Bucharest	Lisbon	Stockholm
Budapest	Liverpool	Strasbourg
Cairo	Ljubljana	St Petersburg
Cape Town	London	Tallinn
Cardiff	Los Angeles	Tirana
Cologne	Lyon	Tokyo
Copenhagen	Madrid	Toulouse
Cork	Marrakech	Turin
Dubai	Marseilles	Valencia
Dublin	Milan	Venice
Dubrovnik	Monte Carlo	Verona
Düsseldorf	Moscow	Vienna
Edinburgh	Munich	Vilnius
Fez	Naples	Warsaw
Florence	New York City	Zagreb
Frankfurt	Nice	Zurich

Available from all good bookshops, your local Thomas Cook travel store or browse and buy online at www.thomascookpublishing.com

Thomas Cook Publishing

Editorial/project management: Lisa Plumridge
Copy editor: Paul Hines
Layout/DTP: Alison Rayner

The publishers would like to thank the following individuals
and organisations for supplying their copyright photographs
for this book: Charles Bowman/Pictures Colour Library, pages 23
& 101; Karsten Koch/Phaeno, page 98; Schützenfest Hannover,
page 15; Caroline Jones, all others.

Send your thoughts to
books@thomascook.com

- Found a great bar, club, shop or must-see sight that we don't feature?
- Like to tip us off about any information that needs a little updating?
- Want to tell us what you love about this handy little guidebook and
  more importantly how we can make it even handier?

Then here's your chance to tell all! Send us ideas, discoveries and
recommendations today and then look out for your valuable input
in the next edition of this title.

Email the above address (stating the title) or write to:
CitySpots Series Editor, Thomas Cook Publishing, PO Box 227,
Coningsby Road, Peterborough PE3 8SB, UK.